THE

DOLLAR

DOOMSDAY

Inside the Coming Global Reset

By Dr. Demoine Kinney
D. Kinney Research Development and Consulting LLC.

Table of Contents

CHAPTER 1

The Dollar Illusion

———————•———————

The dollar has always been more than paper and ink. It has been a promise. A badge of honor, of trust, of power. For over a century, the greenback symbolized stability in a world of chaos. It was the one currency every nation needed, every bank coveted, and every individual believed could buy not only bread but security, freedom, and even dreams.

But promises are fragile. Illusions even more so. What the world sees as a pillar of unshakable value is, in reality, a carefully staged performance—a stage built on debt, deception, and the quiet cooperation of billions who never question the script.

The illusion of the dollar is that it is wealth. The reality is that it is debt, cleverly repackaged as money.

A Brief History of Faith

When Franklin Roosevelt signed the Gold Reserve Act of 1934, seizing the gold of private citizens and tying its value to the Treasury, few Americans understood what was happening. They were told it was necessary to stabilize the nation, to end the Great Depression's stranglehold. And they believed.

Then came Bretton Woods in 1944, when the dollar became the anchor of the postwar world. While Europe lay in ruins and Asia bled from war, America stood tall. The dollar, backed by U.S. gold reserves, became the global measuring stick. Every other currency bent around it. Nations held dollars as treasure, a claim check they could exchange for gold at $35 an ounce.

But illusions are always temporary.

In 1971, Richard Nixon closed the gold window. No more redemption. No more anchors. The dollar was cut loose, floating in the storm of markets, kept afloat not by gold, but by faith—faith in the United States, its economy, and its military might.

This was the great shift: the dollar ceased to be money in the old sense. It became fiat—currency by government decree. Its value was no longer intrinsic. It was psychological.

The illusion solidified: paper was wealth.

The Machinery of Belief

Why did the world accept this? Why did people not rebel against being told that their money, once backed by gold, was now nothing more than promises?

Because the machine was already running.

Banks needed dollars to settle international trade. Oil producers demanded payment in dollars. Governments bought U.S. Treasuries, which were marketed not as debt but as "safe assets." The illusion was reinforced by habit, by inertia, by the subtle hand of financial propaganda that made people believe: "The dollar is money."

And for decades, it worked.

When people in South America, Africa, or Asia lost faith in their own collapsing currencies, they turned not to gold but to dollars. When dictators looted their nations, they stored wealth in offshore dollar accounts. When hedge funds speculated on global markets, they measured profits in dollars.

The dollar wasn't just currency. It was oxygen. And no one questions the air they breathe—until it's poisoned.

The Silent Erosion

But beneath the illusion, rot spread.

The U.S. government discovered it could run deficits without consequence. Trillions borrowed, printed, and injected into the system. Wars in Korea, Vietnam, Iraq, Afghanistan—all funded not by sacrifice but by debt. Social programs, corporate bailouts, stimulus checks—all paid for with the swipe of a digital printing press.

And the world kept buying. Japan, China, Germany, Saudi Arabia—everyone needed dollars, so everyone financed America's illusion.

But here's the truth no politician dares to say: the dollar you hold in your wallet today buys less than it did yesterday, and even less tomorrow. Since 1971, the dollar has lost over 85% of its purchasing power. That is not wealth—it is theft, quietly siphoning the labor of workers, the savings of families, the dreams of generations.

Inflation is not an accident. It is a policy. It is the mechanism by which the illusion is maintained. The dollar illusion tells you that your money is safe, when in fact it is eroding beneath your feet.

Confidence as Currency

Here's the dark secret: the dollar has value only because people believe it does. Confidence is the currency.

When foreign investors buy U.S. bonds, they are not buying assets—they are buying the illusion of stability. When corporations hold cash reserves in dollars, they are not holding wealth—they are holding faith.

But confidence is fragile. It does not erode slowly like stone; it shatters like glass.

Consider a thought experiment: tomorrow morning, China announces it will no longer accept U.S. dollars for trade, switching to a basket of currencies and gold. Saudi Arabia declares oil contracts will now be priced in yuan and euros. Germany proposes a "digital mark" for European energy trades.

What happens?

The illusion vanishes. Overnight, the dollar becomes ordinary paper, no different than the Argentine peso or the Zimbabwean dollar. America's privilege of printing the world's reserve currency collapses, and with it, the empire built on endless debt.

The illusion is maintained by force, by persuasion, by habit. But illusions, once broken, cannot be repaired.

The Dollar as a Weapon

What makes the illusion dangerous is not just that it hides fragility—it hides aggression. The U.S. uses the dollar not only as money but as a weapon.

Sanctions, banking restrictions, frozen assets—all rely on dollar dominance. Nations that disobey Washington find themselves cut off from the global system, suffocated by their dependence on dollars. Iran knows this. Russia knows this. Venezuela knows this.

But each sanction, each weaponized use of the dollar, carries a hidden cost: it teaches the world to build alternatives. To bypass the dollar. To prepare for the day when the illusion fails.

The more the dollar is used as a hammer, the more nations build walls against it. And those walls are rising faster than Washington dares to admit.

The Coming Reckoning

The illusion cannot last forever. It is already cracking. Inflation surges, deficits balloon, political chaos erodes trust. Foreign central banks diversify, stockpiling gold, buying yuan, experimenting with digital currencies.

The world sees the magician's trick, even if Americans do not. They see the dollar for what it is: not wealth, not safety, not freedom—but debt wrapped in green paper.

And when the curtain finally falls, the audience will gasp—not at the collapse itself, but at how long they believed the illusion.

The dollar illusion is not just the story of America's currency; it is the story of every empire that believed it could cheat the laws of economics forever. Like Rome's denarius, like Britain's pound, the dollar too will face its day of reckoning. And when it does, the world will discover that what they thought was money was never money at all—it was only trust. And trust, once lost, is never regained.

CHAPTER 2

Printing the Empire

———————•———————

Empires are not built by soldiers alone. They are built with money. Every empire in history—Rome, Spain, Britain, and now America—has sustained its reach not simply by force, but by financing force. Roads, fleets, armies, fortresses, trade routes—all required treasure. And when the treasure ran out, every empire found the same tool: the printing press.

The dollar empire is no different. Its legions may wear business suits instead of armor, and its warships may carry missiles instead of catapults, but the mechanism is identical. When the gold runs short, when the taxes cannot cover the ambition, when the empire cannot shrink without collapsing—the printing press roars to life.

The illusion of the dollar was the foundation. The printing press is the engine.

From Gold to Paper

In the early 20th century, the United States was the world's creditor. Gold filled its vaults. Foreign nations owed it debts from wars and reconstruction. The dollar's strength was unquestioned, not because of faith alone, but because of metal—real, physical gold bars stacked in Fort Knox.

But wars are greedy beasts. World War I, then World War II, drained treasuries across the globe. Nations printed to survive, their currencies devalued, their gold shipped to America. By 1945, the U.S. held more than two-thirds of the world's gold reserves. The dollar became the measuring stick of the world.

Then came the slow betrayal.

Printing began not as deception but as necessity. America wanted to fund highways, schools, a booming middle class, and later, Vietnam. Taxes couldn't keep up. Gold couldn't be mined fast enough. So Washington turned to the Federal Reserve—the printing press disguised as a central bank.

When Nixon finally cut the last tether to gold in 1971, the empire discovered its ultimate weapon: limitless money. Dollars could be conjured from thin air, debts sold to investors, deficits ignored.

The dollar was no longer backed by gold. It was backed by nothing but Washington's word. And Washington never promised restraint.

War Without Sacrifice

For centuries, war was a tax on nations. Kings raised armies by emptying their treasuries or taxing their people. The cost was visible. Painful. And therefore limited.

But fiat printing changed everything.

Vietnam was funded not by sacrifice but by deficit. Iraq and Afghanistan were financed not by war bonds, but by an invisible tax called inflation. The American people fought wars without ever being asked to pay for them. They swiped credit cards, bought new homes, filled shopping carts, all while their government ran trillion-dollar deficits in the background.

It was the greatest trick in history: a war machine on layaway. Bombs today, payment tomorrow.

Empires fall when their people feel the weight of conquest. But what happens when they don't? Printing allowed America to sustain its empire far longer than any nation in history. Rome debased silver coins until they were worthless. America debases paper until it is indistinguishable from monopoly money—but hides the decay behind statistics, indexes, and economic jargon.

The empire has no need for citizens' permission when it can pay with promises.

The Petrodollar Arrangement

Printing money without consequences requires demand. And demand requires control.

After the gold standard collapsed, Washington struck a silent deal with Riyadh: oil, the lifeblood of the world, would be priced exclusively in U.S. dollars. In exchange, America guaranteed Saudi security.

This single arrangement cemented the printing empire. Nations needed oil. To buy oil, they needed dollars. To get dollars, they bought U.S. debt. Thus, every barrel of oil drilled in the deserts of Arabia translated into global demand for green paper rolling off the Fed's presses.

It was brilliant. It was ruthless. It was imperial finance at its finest.

The petrodollar became the hidden backbone of American power. It allowed the U.S. to print endlessly, knowing that every nation—friend or foe—would have no choice but to absorb the paper. Dollars became the bloodstream of the global economy. Washington could export inflation abroad, soaking the world in green ink while keeping its own system alive.

The empire didn't just print money. It printed obedience.

The Hidden Tax: Inflation

Every empire hides its theft behind complexity. Rome mixed base metals into coins. Britain clipped the edges of silver. America prints digital money and calls it stimulus.

Inflation is the tax no one votes for, the theft no one sees. When Washington prints, the value of every existing dollar falls. The worker saving for retirement, the family budgeting for groceries, the student paying tuition—they pay the bill.

The empire thrives on this hidden tax. Politicians claim to raise wages, to grow wealth, to expand opportunity. But the printing press ensures that every dollar earned tomorrow is weaker than the dollar spent today.

This is how empires hollow from within. Not by conquest abroad, but by corrosion at home. The printing press fuels expansion while quietly devouring its own citizens' prosperity.

The dollar empire tells its people they are rich. But their wealth is slipping through their fingers, replaced by paper promises that buy less each year.

The Central Bank Alchemy

The Federal Reserve is the high priest of this system, cloaked in secrecy and jargon. It speaks of "quantitative easing," "liquidity injections," and "balance sheets." But strip away the language, and the truth is primitive: they print.

In 2008, during the global financial crisis, the printing press went into overdrive. Trillions were conjured to bail out banks, prop up markets, and calm panic. In 2020, amid a pandemic, the Fed unleashed even more— showering Wall Street and Washington alike with freshly minted dollars.

The empire's lifeline is no longer productivity or innovation—it is the central bank's willingness to print.

But every dose of printing is like heroin. Relief at first. Dependency next. Collapse in the end. The empire cannot stop printing without triggering a crash. And it cannot continue printing without destroying its currency.

This is the fatal trap.

The Mirage of Wealth

Visit New York, Los Angeles, Miami—skyscrapers rise, luxury cars cruise, markets boom. On the surface, the empire appears rich beyond measure. But look deeper.

Beneath the gloss lies debt: government debt, corporate debt, household debt. Trillions piled upon trillions, sustained only because the Fed can print endlessly. Americans do not live in wealth—they live in credit. Their prosperity is not earned—it is borrowed.

This is the mirage of the printing empire: wealth without substance, prosperity without foundation. And mirages vanish when the sun shifts.

The Cracks Begin to Show

For decades, printing seemed harmless. Inflation was "low." The dollar was "stable." The empire appeared unshakable.

But now, the cracks widen.

Nations diversify away from the dollar. Central banks hoard gold again. Cryptocurrencies challenge fiat's monopoly. Inflation surges past official lies. Confidence erodes.

The printing press, once the empire's engine, has become its addiction. And every addict faces the same ending: destruction by the very substance that sustained them.

The dollar empire was not built on strength, but on printing. And what printing gives, printing can take away. For every empire that believed it could conjure wealth from thin air discovered the same truth: the bill always comes due. America is no exception. The presses may roar, but they cannot drown out the sound of history repeating.

CHAPTER 3

The Debt Machine

————————•————————

Debt is the oxygen of the modern empire. It flows unseen, filling every lung, every bank account, every nation's balance sheet. Americans wake up in homes bought with mortgages, drive cars paid for with loans, study in schools financed with borrowed tuition, and buy their groceries with credit cards. Corporations expand not with profits but with leverage. Governments govern not with taxes but with deficits.

The United States does not run on productivity alone. It runs on the Debt Machine—a vast, humming apparatus that churns out promises, IOUs, and contracts at a speed no nation in history has ever dared.

The illusion of money was one trick. The printing press was another. But the true genius—and the fatal flaw—of the dollar empire is that its very survival depends on debt. Without it, the system collapses. With it, the collapse is only delayed.

The Birth of the Machine

Before the 20th century, debt was shameful. Families avoided it. Politicians feared it. Nations collapsed under its weight. But somewhere along the way, debt transformed from vice to virtue.

After World War II, America was the creditor of the world. Other nations owed it money. Its citizens lived modestly, saving more than they spent. But then came the cultural shift: television ads selling the American Dream, banks offering easy credit, politicians promising prosperity without sacrifice.

The machine was born when the government discovered it could run deficits indefinitely, and banks discovered they could profit from lending endlessly. Together, they rewired the economy. Savings declined. Borrowing soared.

Debt became not a burden but a business.

Government by Deficit

Every year, Washington spends more than it collects. Politicians promise lower taxes and higher benefits. Wars, bailouts, healthcare, welfare, infrastructure—everything is financed not with revenue but with borrowing.

This is the central lie of modern democracy: that you can have everything without paying for it.

In the 1960s, deficits were measured in billions. By the 1980s, in hundreds of billions. Today, trillions are added yearly, stacked on top of a mountain that already towers above the nation. Over $34 trillion in official debt, and climbing. Unfunded liabilities—Social Security, Medicare, pensions—push the real figure beyond $100 trillion.

This is not budgeting. It is insolvency masked by printing. The Debt Machine ensures politicians can spend without consequence, pushing the pain onto future generations.

But the future always arrives.

The Consumer's Chains

It is not only the government that is enslaved. The American citizen is shackled to the Debt Machine.

Mortgages: thirty-year chains binding workers to banks. Student loans: lifelong anchors dragging graduates into decades of repayment. Credit cards: revolving traps with interest rates that quietly bleed families dry.

The illusion tells Americans they are homeowners. In truth, the banks own the homes until the final payment. The illusion tells students they are investing in their future. In truth, many buy worthless degrees with debts they will never escape. The illusion tells consumers they are free to buy now and pay later. In truth, they are indentured servants to financial institutions.

The Debt Machine does not empower—it enslaves. And the more it enslaves, the more it grows.

Corporate Junkies

Corporations, too, are addicted. Once, profits fueled expansion. Today, debt fuels stock buybacks, mergers, and executive bonuses.

Wall Street doesn't ask whether a company is profitable. It asks whether it can borrow cheaply. Fortune 500 giants gorge on bonds, borrowing billions to inflate share prices. Zombies—companies that cannot survive without constant borrowing—now stagger across the economy, kept alive by artificially low interest rates.

The illusion of corporate strength masks fragility. These titans stand not on solid balance sheets but on mountains of leverage. When interest rates rise, when cash flow falters, the zombies fall. And when they fall, they drag the markets—and the middle class pensions tied to them—into the abyss.

The Debt Machine feeds them, but also ensures their destruction.

The Global Trap

America's debt addiction would have killed any other nation long ago. But the dollar's status as the world's reserve currency created a global trap.

Foreign nations buy U.S. Treasuries not because they want to, but because they must. To settle trade, to stabilize currencies, to maintain reserves, they lend money to Washington. China, Japan, Europe, oil states—all finance America's deficits by recycling their dollar surpluses into U.S. bonds.

It is the perfect scam: America spends recklessly, and the world funds its excess. But every scam ends. Foreigners are waking up. They see the mountain of debt. They see the inflation eroding their returns. They see the empire weaponizing the dollar.

The trap is breaking. And when it snaps, the Debt Machine will devour its master.

Interest: The Hidden Fuse

Debt alone does not kill. It is interesting that detonates the bomb.

As long as rates were near zero, the machine could hum. The government borrowed trillions with minimal cost. Corporations rolled over loans cheaply. Consumers refinanced mortgages endlessly.

But when interest rises, the gears grind. Suddenly, Washington's debt service consumes the budget. Corporations face bankruptcy. Families lose homes.

Interest is the fuse that turns debt from illusion to catastrophe. And the fuse is already lit.

The Psychology of Enslavement

Debt is not merely financial. It is psychological. It teaches citizens to obey.

A worker with a paid-off home can walk away from a bad job. A worker drowning in debt cannot. A nation free of deficits can choose its destiny. A nation chained to creditors cannot.

The Debt Machine is not just an economic system—it is a system of control. Citizens who believe they own wealth are less likely to rebel, even when that "wealth" is only borrowed. Nations that rely on dollar debt are less likely to defy America, even when resentment grows.

Debt pacifies. Debt enslaves. Debt maintains the illusion of freedom while ensuring obedience.

The Collapse of the Machine

Every machine breaks. Rome's silver coins became worthless. Spain's empire collapsed under debts from endless wars. Britain's pound sterling lost its crown after two world wars it could not afford.

America's Debt Machine is no different.

The numbers no longer add up. Trillions upon trillions of debt cannot be repaid, only rolled over. The interest burden is exploding. Inflation surges as printing accelerates. The foreign creditors withdraw. Confidence erodes.

The collapse will not be gradual. It will be sudden. Confidence will shatter, markets will panic, and the machine will seize. The empire that believed it could borrow forever will discover that forever always has an end.

The Debt Machine is the heartbeat of the dollar empire. It pumps life into governments, corporations, and citizens alike. But every heartbeat is borrowed time. And when the machine stops, it will not be a slowdown. It will be cardiac arrest—the sudden death of a system that believed debt was wealth.

CHAPTER 4

Inflation Nation

———————•———————

Inflation is the most deceptive crime ever committed against a people. It does not arrive with soldiers. It does not steal with guns. It creeps silently, stripping wealth from pockets, siphoning labor from hands, and stealing futures from children. It is a thief disguised as prosperity, a tax disguised as growth, a weapon disguised as policy.

America has become an Inflation Nation, built on the quiet erosion of value. The empire tells its citizens they are richer than ever, but their dollars buy less every year. The government boasts of higher wages, but groceries and rent consume the gains. Politicians speak of prosperity, while families silently downgrade their lives.

Inflation is not the disease—it is the symptom of a terminal addiction to printing, debt, and deceit. It is the smoke rising from the fire of a collapsing system.

The Myth of "Moderate" Inflation

The Federal Reserve tells Americans that "a little inflation is healthy." Like a doctor prescribing poison, they insist that 2% inflation is necessary for growth.

But consider the math: at 2% inflation, the dollar loses half its value in just 35 years. At 4%, it loses half in 18 years. This is not stability. This is slow-motion robbery.

The myth of "moderate inflation" is propaganda. It conditions citizens to accept the erosion of their savings as normal. It teaches workers to run faster just to stay in place. It convinces investors to gamble on markets rather than save in cash.

The truth is brutal: there is no safe inflation. Every percentage point is theft. And theft compounds over time.

History's Warnings

We have seen this before.

In Weimar Germany, the printing press paid for war reparations until bread cost billions of marks. Families hauled cash in wheelbarrows, only to find it worthless by nightfall. In Zimbabwe, trillion-dollar notes littered the streets, their value evaporated. In Venezuela, bolívar banknotes became cheaper as toilet paper than as currency.

America believes it is immune because it is powerful. But history does not exempt empires—it punishes them. Every hyperinflation began with denial. Every collapse began with leaders insisting the currency was sound.

The warning signs are here: endless printing, soaring deficits, manipulated statistics, and a population forced to spend more for less. America may not yet face wheelbarrows of cash, but the road is the same, and the direction is clear.

The Lie of Statistics

Official numbers are illusions. The Consumer Price Index (CPI), the government's chosen measure of inflation, is a rigged game. Politicians change the formula whenever the truth becomes too ugly.

Food and energy costs—the very items people cannot live without—are often minimized or excluded. "Hedonic adjustments" claim that if a product improves in quality, its rising price does not count as inflation. Substitution tricks say if steak gets too expensive and people buy chicken, the price increase disappears from the index.

This is not measurement. This is manipulation.

The real inflation—the one felt by families at the checkout line, by renters signing leases, by parents paying tuition—is far higher than the official lie. The Inflation Nation survives not only by printing but by concealing the consequences.

Wages vs. Prices: The Rigged Race

Workers celebrate when wages rise. But inflation runs faster. A raise that adds $200 a month vanishes when rent increases $300, gas climbs $50, and groceries another $100.

The empire pretends workers are gaining. In reality, they are treading water in a storm, paddling furiously while the current drags them backward.

This is the cruel genius of inflation: it gives the illusion of progress while guaranteeing decline. The worker works harder, the saver saves longer, the investor risks more—yet all fall behind. Only the Debt Machine gains, because inflation makes debt easier to repay with cheaper dollars.

The system is designed so that the citizen always loses, while the state always wins.

Inflation as Policy

Inflation is not a mistake. It is not mismanagement. It is a deliberate policy.

Every dollar printed reduces the burden of government debt. Every percentage point of inflation steals from savers and transfers wealth to debtors—chief among them, Washington. Politicians will never admit it, but inflation is their lifeline. Without it, the empire collapses under its own obligations.

This is why the Fed cannot—and will not—ever truly end inflation. They may raise rates for a season, crush markets, and pretend to fight. But in the end, they return to printing. Because without inflation, the system suffocates.

The empire requires inflation the way a drowning man requires air. And like a drowning man, it will claw, fight, and destroy anything to keep it flowing.

The Cultural Consequences

Inflation does more than erode money. It erodes society.

When people cannot save, they stop planning for the future. When prices rise faster than wages, families delay children, marriages, and home ownership. When savings vanish, resentment grows, and trust in institutions collapses.

An Inflation Nation is a desperate nation. It produces citizens who gamble on speculative markets, who chase quick profits, who abandon discipline because discipline no longer pays. It breeds cynicism, short-term thinking, and social decay.

The empire believes inflation is economic policy. In truth, it is social sabotage.

The Global Ripple

Because the dollar is the world's reserve currency, inflation does not stay within America's borders. It ripples across oceans, infecting every nation tied to the greenback.

When Washington prints, global food and energy prices rise. Poor nations suffer first. Families in Africa, Asia, and Latin America spend half their income on food. A spike in wheat or rice costs—triggered by dollar inflation—pushes millions into hunger.

Inflation is not just an American crime. It is a global weapon. The Inflation Nation exports misery worldwide, while pretending to offer aid.

The Point of No Return

There is no easy escape from inflation. To kill it, the Fed would need to raise interest rates high enough to crush borrowing, spending, and speculation. But that would collapse the Debt Machine, bankrupt the government, and trigger depression. To ignore it, the Fed must keep printing, which destroys the dollar's value.

This is the trap. There is no third path. The Inflation Nation is locked in a death spiral of its own making.

And the longer it delays the reckoning, the worse the reckoning becomes.

Inflation is not a glitch in the system—it is the system. It is how the empire sustains itself, how it enslaves its citizens, how it exports its decay to the world. But like every parasite, it cannot feed forever without killing its host. America has become an Inflation Nation, and the day is coming when the cost of deception can no longer be hidden.

CHAPTER 5

The Petrodollar's Death Rattle

———————•———————

Every empire has a secret pact, a bargain struck in shadows that sustains its dominance long after its strength should have faded. For Rome, it was the legions securing grain from Egypt. For Britain, it was the Royal Navy ensuring trade routes stayed open. For America, it was the petrodollar—a deal so cunning, so far-reaching, that it extended the dollar's life by half a century.

But like every bargain with history, it carries an expiration date. And that date is fast approaching.

The petrodollar system is dying. And when it breathes its last, the world will not merely witness a change in markets. It will witness the collapse of the empire's foundation.

The Deal That Changed the World

It began in the 1970s, after Nixon severed the last tie between the dollar and gold. The greenback floated untethered, its value uncertain, its credibility shaken. The empire needed a new anchor—not metal, but demand.

So Washington turned to Riyadh.

In 1974, the United States struck a deal with Saudi Arabia: in exchange for American protection and military support, the Saudis agreed to sell their oil exclusively in U.S. dollars. Other OPEC nations soon followed.

This single agreement reshaped global finance. Oil is the lifeblood of modern civilization. Every nation needs it. And if oil is priced in dollars, then every nation needs dollars.

Thus, the "petrodollar" was born.

From that moment, the dollar was not merely a currency. It was a ticket to energy. A passcode to survival. Nations scrambled to acquire dollars, not out of loyalty to Washington, but out of necessity. To buy oil, you needed dollars. To earn dollars, you had to trade with America or buy its debt.

The empire had discovered alchemy: it could print the very currency the world needed to keep its lights on.

The Silent Tribute System

The petrodollar turned the globe into a tributary system. Just as ancient empires demanded gold and silver from their vassals, America demanded dollars—but with one crucial difference: the vassals created the demand themselves.

Japan needed oil. So Japan bought dollars, then bought U.S. Treasuries to hold them. Europe needed oil. So Europe bought dollars, then reinvested in American banks. Even rivals like China and Russia were forced to accumulate dollar reserves, simply to keep their economies running.

This flow of money back into America's coffers was called "petrodollar recycling." Oil producers deposited their profits into U.S. banks. Foreign nations reinvested their surpluses in U.S. debt. The machine fed itself.

Washington could run deficits forever, and the world would finance them. Trillions printed, borrowed, and spent—all sustained by the simple fact that every drop of oil traded in the world had to pass through the greenback.

The petrodollar wasn't just an agreement. It was a tribute disguised as trade.

Weaponizing the System

The petrodollar gave Washington more than wealth. It gave it power.

With the dollar as the world's energy currency, America controlled the global financial plumbing. Any nation that dared step out of line could be cut off from the system. Iran learned this when sanctions locked it out of dollar transactions. Venezuela learned it when its oil exports were strangled. Russia learned it when its banks were frozen out of SWIFT.

The dollar became not just money, but a weapon—bloodless yet devastating. America could bankrupt adversaries without firing a shot.

But this weapon carried a hidden cost: it made the system fragile. Each sanction, each act of financial warfare, drove nations to seek alternatives. Each punishment chipped away at the illusion of permanence.

The petrodollar's dominance was never eternal. And Washington's overreach hastened its demise.

The Rise of Rivals

For decades, no challenger could dislodge the dollar. But the 21st century changed the landscape.

China rose to industrial supremacy, building Belt and Road alliances across Asia, Africa, and beyond. Russia, rich in natural gas and oil, forged energy partnerships with Europe and China. Together, they began whispering the unthinkable: trade without the dollar.

In 2014, after sanctions over Crimea, Russia and China signed agreements to settle energy trades in rubles and yuan. By the 2020s, those whispers grew into policy. Saudi Arabia began accepting yuan for oil. BRICS nations openly discussed creating alternative currencies. Central banks worldwide accelerated gold purchases, hedging against a dollar collapse.

The once-unquestioned petrodollar faced rivals—not in theory, but in practice.

The death rattle had begun.

The Domino Effect

The petrodollar's collapse will not be gradual. It will be sudden, like a dam breaking.

Imagine this: Saudi Arabia officially announces oil contracts in yuan, euros, and digital currencies. Other OPEC members follow. China, the world's largest oil importer, no longer needs dollars for energy. Russia trades oil and gas in rubles and yuan. India settles with Gulf states in rupees.

Suddenly, the demand for dollars evaporates. Central banks dump Treasuries. Foreign nations repatriate reserves. The recycling machine shuts down.

Trillions of dollars come rushing home, no longer needed abroad. Inflation erupts. Interest rates skyrocket. The empire, once sustained by tribute, finds itself drowning in its own currency.

This is not speculation. The groundwork is already laid. The only question is when the final domino falls.

The Illusion of Control

Washington insists the dollar will remain supreme. Its officials laugh at the idea of rivals replacing it. They point to the size of U.S. markets, the depth of its financial system, and the safety of its bonds.

But this is arrogance—the same arrogance every empire displayed before its fall. The Romans mocked the "barbarians." The British dismissed the dollar in the 1920s. America now sneers at the yuan, the ruble, and gold.

The empire forgets that dominance is not about logic—it is about trust. And trust is eroding faster than Washington can print.

The petrodollar's death rattle is not about economics alone. It is about psychology. Once the world believes the dollar is replaceable, the dollar *is* replaceable.

The Endgame

When the petrodollar dies, the consequences will be immediate and devastating:

- **Collapse of foreign demand for U.S. debt.** Washington will no longer sell its IOUs abroad with ease.

- **Surge of dollars returning home.** Inflation will explode as excess currency floods domestic markets.

- **Geopolitical realignment.** Nations once bound by dollar dependence will align with China, Russia, and alternative systems.

- **Loss of empire.** Without the ability to finance deficits effortlessly, America will be forced to retrench, retreat, and face realities it has avoided for decades.

The death rattle of the petrodollar is not just the end of a system. It is the end of an era—the twilight of dollar hegemony.

The petrodollar was the empire's secret pact, its invisible empire of oil and paper. But pacts built on necessity, not loyalty, cannot last. As nations awaken and alliances shift, the death rattle grows louder. And when the final breath escapes, the empire will discover what it means to pay for power in a world no longer willing to subsidize its illusion.

CHAPTER 6

The China Factor

———————•———————

Every empire falls because another rises to challenge it. Rome had the Goths. Britain had America. And now America has China.

The challenge is not military—at least not yet. It is economical. It is financial. It is strategic. China is not trying to defeat the dollar on the battlefield. It is trying to strangle it in the marketplace.

The United States built its empire on consumption and debt. China is building its empire on production and patience. Where Washington prints, Beijing builds. Where America consumes, China invests. Where the dollar demands obedience, the yuan quietly offers alternatives.

The China Factor is not just competition. It is the slow, deliberate construction of a parallel system—a system designed to make the dollar obsolete.

Made in China, Paid in Yuan

For decades, the world depended on America's consumer markets. Cheap goods flowed into Walmart, Target, and Amazon, stamped "Made in China." The U.S. exported dollars, China exported everything else.

This arrangement gave China two weapons: mountains of dollar reserves and leverage over supply chains. Factories in Guangzhou, Shenzhen, and Wuhan didn't just produce cheap toys and electronics—they produced dependence. American corporations hollowed out their own industries, trading sovereignty for profits, while China amassed financial and industrial dominance.

But Beijing didn't stop at production. It began pushing for payment in yuan. From oil to minerals to manufactured goods, China steadily chipped away at the dollar's monopoly. Its message to the world was subtle but clear: "You no longer need America's currency to survive."

The more nations trade in yuan, the less oxygen the dollar breathes.

The Belt and Road Web

If the petrodollar was Washington's hidden pact, the Belt and Road Initiative (BRI) is Beijing's counterpact.

Launched in 2013, BRI is more than infrastructure. It is empire-building by asphalt and steel. Railways across Central Asia, ports in Africa, highways in Europe, digital networks in Latin America—all financed by Chinese banks, built by Chinese companies, and denominated in yuan.

This is how China extends its influence: not by conquest, but by construction. Each bridge, each power plant, each fiber optic cable is a chain binding nations to Beijing's orbit. And with every project, the dollar loses ground.

Nations indebted to China do not need U.S. dollars to repay loans—they need yuan. The Belt and Road is not just reshaping trade routes. It is reshaping the financial bloodstream of the planet.

The Yuan's Quiet Rise

Skeptics laugh at the idea of the yuan replacing the dollar. They say China's currency is not "free-floating," that its financial system is opaque, that investors lack trust. They said the same about the dollar once.

China is playing a long game. It doesn't need to dethrone the dollar overnight. It only needs to make the yuan credible enough to compete. Step by step, it is succeeding:

- **Currency Swaps:** China has signed bilateral agreements with dozens of nations, allowing them to trade in yuan directly.

- **Digital Yuan:** Beijing is pioneering central bank digital currency (CBDC) technology, creating a tool for seamless global transactions outside the dollar system.

- **Gold Backing:** China quietly buys thousands of tons of gold, signaling that its currency may one day be tied not to promises but to metal.

- **Oil and Gas Trades:** In deals with Russia, Iran, and even Saudi Arabia, China is paying for energy in yuan.

The yuan does not need to replace the dollar everywhere. It only needs to weaken it in enough places to shatter the illusion of supremacy.

The Dollar's Addiction, China's Patience

America lives in the present. Its political cycles last four years. Its markets obsess over quarterly earnings. Its citizens demand instant gratification.

China has lived for centuries. Its leaders think in dynasties, not elections. Its strategy is not about next week's headlines but the next generation's supremacy.

This is the fatal mismatch: the dollar empire is addicted to immediacy, while China is patient. America borrows and prints to keep its system afloat today. China invests and waits for tomorrow.

Empires built on debt cannot outlast empires built on patience.

Financial Warfare Without Bullets

China does not need to fire missiles to weaken America. It simply needs to dump U.S. debt.

Beijing holds over $800 billion in U.S. Treasuries. If it liquidated them suddenly, markets would convulse, interest rates would soar, and Washington would face financial chaos. Even gradual selling undermines confidence, signaling to the world that the largest creditor is abandoning the system.

But China's real weapon is not what it sells. It is what it builds. Every yuan-denominated trade deal, every Belt and Road project, every digital currency experiment chips away at dollar demand. America relies on the world needing dollars. China's mission is to make that need vanish.

This is financial warfare—bloodless, silent, and devastating.

The BRICS Counterweight

China is not acting alone. Alongside Russia, India, Brazil, and South Africa, it has forged the BRICS alliance. Once dismissed as symbolic, BRICS now challenges the very foundation of the dollar system.

At recent summits, BRICS nations have openly discussed creating a shared currency, backed by commodities or gold. They have expanded membership to include major oil producers, tightening their grip on global resources.

This is the nightmare scenario for Washington: a coalition of rising powers, united not by ideology but by necessity, working together to bypass the dollar.

China is the engine of this coalition. Without it, BRICS is a talking shop. With it, BRICS is a revolution.

The U.S. Response: Denial and Decay

Washington knows China is a threat. But its responses are clumsy and self-defeating. Trade wars, tariffs, and sanctions have only driven Beijing to deepen ties with Russia, Africa, and Latin America. Efforts to isolate China technologically have accelerated its domestic innovation. Attempts to contain it militarily have only exposed America's overstretched empire.

The dollar empire cannot outbuild China, cannot outwait China, and increasingly cannot outcompete China. Its only weapon is the same it has used for decades: printing.

But printing is a weakness, not strength. And China knows it.

The Coming Confrontation

The China Factor is not about if, but when. The world is shifting. The yuan is rising. The petrodollar is rattling. The debt machine is creaking. Inflation is surging. Confidence is cracking.

The confrontation will not begin with tanks in Taiwan or missiles in the Pacific. It will begin with an announcement, quiet but earth-shattering:

"From this day forward, oil contracts between Beijing and Riyadh will be settled in yuan."

That moment will mark the turning point. The dollar's illusion will shatter. The empire will stumble. And the China Factor will become the China Reality.

China is not racing against America—it is waiting for America to collapse under its own weight. And when the dollar falls, China will not need to strike a blow. It will simply step into the vacuum, offering the world what America can no longer provide: stability, discipline, and an alternative to an empire that mistook arrogance for eternity.

CHAPTER 7

Bank Runs in the Digital Age

———————●———————

Banking has always been a business of confidence. Your money is not in the vault; it is lent out, invested, leveraged. The bank holds a fraction, a thin layer of reserves, and prays you never ask for more than that. As long as everyone believes, the system works. But belief is fragile. The moment people doubt, they run. And when they run, the bank collapses.

This has been true since the Medici ran banks in Renaissance Florence. It was true in 1929 when panicked crowds gathered outside failing banks. It was true in 2008 when Lehman Brothers imploded.

But today, the run is different. Faster. Ruthless. Invisible.

We live in an era where a single tweet, a viral video, or a rumor in a WhatsApp group can erase a bank overnight. The bank run has entered the digital age. And in this age, the dollar system is more vulnerable than ever.

The Anatomy of a Classic Bank Run

To understand the danger, consider the old version.

In the Great Depression, customers heard whispers that their bank might be insolvent. They lined up outside the branch, demanding withdrawals. Photographs of desperate crowds reinforced the panic. One failure triggered another. Thousands of banks collapsed.

The system was slow. News traveled by word of mouth or newspapers. Withdrawals required cashiers and tellers. Collapse took days or weeks. The government had time—sometimes—to intervene.

Today, none of those buffers exist.

The Speed of Panic

When Silicon Valley Bank collapsed in 2023, it wasn't because lines stretched around the block. It was because billions of dollars were withdrawn with a few keystrokes. Tech executives sent Slack messages. Investors tweeted warnings. Within 48 hours, $42 billion evaporated from the bank's deposits. No lines. No waiting. Just money vanishing into the digital ether.

This was a glimpse of the future. In an interconnected, smartphone-dominated world, panic is instantaneous. A whisper can circle the globe in minutes. Fear can become a self-fulfilling prophecy before regulators even know what happened.

The bank run has become a viral phenomenon.

Social Media as the Spark

The new bank run does not begin at the teller's window. It begins on social media.

A tweet from a hedge fund. A viral TikTok video showing a "bank in trouble." A leaked email shared on Telegram. Suddenly, millions of people doubt their money is safe. And doubt spreads faster than any bank can process withdrawals.

Banks used to die in silence. Today, they die in trending hashtags.

The illusion of stability cannot survive the velocity of information.

The Digital Dollar Drain

Here lies the empire's deeper vulnerability. The U.S. banking system is a spiderweb of leverage. Trillions in deposits, trillions more in loans, and only a fraction in actual cash. The system works only if people stay calm.

But what happens when calm is impossible? What happens when, in a moment of global panic, millions of depositors in dozens of banks hit "transfer" at once?

Money does not trickle out anymore—it floods. Within hours, banks collapse like dominoes. The Federal Reserve cannot respond fast enough. FDIC insurance becomes irrelevant. The illusion of stability dissolves in real time.

This is the nightmare of the digital age: a nationwide—or global—bank run that moves faster than governments can contain.

Central Banks on the Edge

The Federal Reserve knows this risk. That's why it moves toward **Central Bank Digital Currencies (CBDCs)**. Officials sell them as innovation, efficiency, and modernization. In reality, CBDCs are a survival strategy.

In a CBDC system, your money is not in a bank. It is in the central bank's ledger. No more private banks failing. No more runs. The government controls the flow directly.

But the cure is worse than the disease. A CBDC system gives the state total surveillance and control. Every transaction is tracked. Every purchase is monitored. Every account is switchable on or off.

The bank run may be prevented—but freedom dies with it.

The Chain Reaction

Imagine this scenario:

A geopolitical shock erupts—perhaps Taiwan, perhaps the Middle East. Markets shudder. A rumor spreads that a major U.S. bank is insolvent. Within minutes, deposits flee. Billions shift into treasuries, crypto, or gold. Screens across the world flash red.

The Fed intervenes, promising backstops. But faith erodes. Foreign investors dump dollars, fearing contagion. The stock market plummets. The dollar weakens. Confidence—the only true currency—evaporates.

By nightfall, the panic spreads globally. Banks in Europe face outflows. Asian markets crash. A global dollar run has begun—not just on a single bank, but on the system itself.

This is not fantasy. It is the logical conclusion of a fragile empire wired into a world where information cannot be contained.

The Illusion of Safety Nets

Politicians reassure citizens: "Your deposits are safe. FDIC insurance protects you."

But FDIC insurance is a mirage. The insurance fund is minuscule compared to the scale of deposits. If a handful of regional banks fail, it works. If the system itself fails, it is meaningless.

The government promises bailouts. But bailouts are just printed by another name. And printing in the middle of a digital bank run does not restore confidence—it accelerates inflation, feeding the very fire that sparked the panic.

The safety nets exist only as long as people do not use them. The moment they are tested, they tear.

Global Contagion

The danger is not confined to America. The dollar is the backbone of global banking. European banks hold dollar reserves. Asian corporations borrow in dollars. Emerging markets rely on dollar liquidity.

A digital-age bank run in the U.S. is not a local problem. It is a global contagion. Within hours, markets from Frankfurt to Shanghai tremble. Nations scramble to defend their currencies. Central banks intervene frantically.

Confidence, once global, collapses globally. The illusion of dollar supremacy dies not in a single nation, but everywhere at once.

The End of Trust

In the end, the bank run is not about money. It is about trust.

When people believe their deposits are safe, they remain. When they doubt, they flee. In the digital age, doubt spreads like wildfire. No walls, no regulators, no interventions can contain it.

The dollar empire survives on confidence alone. But confidence, once shattered, cannot be restored.

The bank run of the digital age will not be a trickle of depositors in line outside a branch. It will be a flood of withdrawals moving at the speed of light, invisible until it is unstoppable. And when that day comes, the dollar empire will discover that its greatest strength—technology—has become its executioner.

CHAPTER 8

Wall Street's Hidden
Derivatives Bomb

———————•———————

If debt is the oxygen of the empire, derivatives are its dynamite.

They are invisible to the average citizen. They are buried in financial reports no one reads. They are disguised in jargon that even regulators cannot decipher. But they exist—and they are vast.

Derivatives are bets. Contracts built on contracts. Layers of speculation stacked on top of real assets until the original foundation disappears. A mortgage becomes a bond. That bond becomes a collateralized debt obligation (CDO). That CDO becomes a derivative on a derivative. Trillions pile upon trillions, each bet tied to the next, until the system resembles not a fortress but a house of cards.

The numbers are staggering. By conservative estimates, the global derivatives market exceeds **$600 trillion**. Some analysts put it at **over $1 quadrillion**—more than ten times the GDP of the entire planet.

Wall Street calls it "risk management." In reality, it is the largest financial bomb ever assembled. And the timer is ticking.

The Casino Disguised as Finance

Derivatives were sold as tools of safety. Banks claimed they reduced risk, spreading exposure across markets. In truth, they multiplied risk, scattering it like shrapnel across the globe.

At their core, derivatives are casino chips. A farmer hedging wheat prices is one thing. But Wall Street turned hedging into gambling. Banks bet on mortgages, currencies, interest rates, oil prices, credit defaults—anything with a pulse.

Each bet seemed harmless. But when bets connect across institutions, across nations, across markets, the web becomes lethal. One default cascades into dozens, then hundreds. The system cannot absorb the shock.

This is what happened in 2008. Mortgage derivatives imploded. Lehman Brothers collapsed. AIG nearly died. Trillions vanished. The system teetered. And that was just a fragment of the derivative bomb.

The Illusion of Control

After 2008, politicians promised reform. They spoke of "too big to fail," of transparency, of regulation. But Wall Street is cleverer than Washington. The bomb was not dismantled—it was hidden deeper.

Today, derivatives are even larger, even more complex. Banks shift them into "off-balance-sheet" entities. Regulators nod, pretending the danger is contained. But the danger has not shrunk—it has metastasized.

The illusion is that regulators can monitor the system. The reality is that no one, not even the bankers themselves, fully understands the web they've spun. The derivatives bomb is too large, too complex, too opaque to defuse.

The Interest Rate Trigger

Every bomb has a trigger. For derivatives, it is interest rates.

For years, Wall Street thrived on near-zero rates. Bets were made assuming cheap money forever. Leverage piled higher and higher. But when rates rise—as they have in recent years—the entire equation shifts.

A slight increase in interest rates alters the value of trillions in derivative contracts. Margins must be posted. Collateral must be raised. Suddenly, banks scramble for liquidity. What seemed like "manageable risk" became a liquidity crisis.

This is the silent trigger embedded in the system. A single rate hike can set off chain reactions no one anticipates.

The Counterparty Nightmare

Derivatives rely on counterparties—two sides of a bet. If one side fails, the other side is left holding the bag.

This is what made AIG so catastrophic in 2008. It had written billions in credit default swaps—insurance on bad mortgages. When those mortgages collapsed, AIG couldn't pay. The government bailed it out, not to save AIG, but to save the counterparties who would have collapsed with it.

Today, the same nightmare exists, only bigger. If a major bank fails, its counterparties fail too. The shock spreads instantly through the global web. What begins as a single failure becomes systemic collapse.

The bomb is not just big—it is interconnected. One spark ignites the whole network.

The Illusion of "Netting"

Wall Street insists the bomb is smaller than it looks. They claim "netting" reduces exposure—that if Bank A owes Bank B $10 trillion and Bank B owes Bank A $9 trillion, the risk is only $1 trillion.

This is fantasy. Netting works only if everyone pays. In a crisis, counterparties default. The $10 trillion liability is real. The $9 trillion asset is worthless. Netting collapses under stress, leaving the raw exposure intact.

The derivatives bomb cannot be wished away by accounting tricks.

Derivatives and the Dollar

Why does this matter for the dollar? Because the bomb is priced in dollars.

The vast majority of global derivatives are denominated in the greenback. This gives the illusion of strength—the world still uses the dollar as its unit of settlement. But it also creates fragility.

If confidence in the dollar falters, if foreign nations flee the currency, the entire derivatives market trembles. Collateral calls explode. Banks scramble for dollars. The system chokes.

In this way, the derivatives bomb and the dollar are chained together. If one collapses, the other follows.

The Unspoken Fear

Bankers never admit the risk. Politicians never discuss it. The public never hears of it. But behind closed doors, every central banker, every finance minister, every Wall Street CEO knows the truth:

The derivatives market is unbacked, uncontrolled, and unsustainable.

The entire global economy rests on a bomb so large it defies imagination. And unlike nuclear bombs, this one has no deterrent. Its detonation is not a matter of "if," but "when."

The Day It Blows

Picture the moment.

A hedge fund fails after a miscalculated interest rate bet. Its losses ripple to counterparties. A European bank collapses. Panic spreads to New York.

Liquidity evaporates. Derivative contracts worth trillions are suddenly in default.

Markets crash. Governments scramble to print. Central banks coordinate emergency bailouts. But the hole is too deep. Confidence evaporates.

The dollar, tied to this system, plunges in value. Inflation surges as printing accelerates. Citizens watch savings vanish. Nations once loyal to the dollar flee.

The derivatives bomb detonates—not with an explosion, but with a chain reaction of defaults that collapses the illusion of stability.

Wall Street built a bomb too big to contain, too complex to defuse, and too dangerous to ignore. It hides in plain sight, humming beneath the surface of the dollar empire. And when it detonates, it will not just destroy banks or markets—it will destroy faith in the very currency that sustains the illusion of American power.

CHAPTER 9

The Day the Dollar Died

———————•———————

History is usually written in decades, sometimes years. But collapses are written in hours.

Rome did not fall in a single day, but the sack of the city happened in one. The British pound did not lose its empire overnight, but its final dethroning came in a weekend crisis in 1949.

And so it will be with the dollar. For years, the cracks have widened— debt, inflation, the petrodollar's decay, the derivatives bomb. But the day the dollar dies will not fade. It will be a shock, a jolt, a convulsion that takes the world from illusion to chaos in less than a week.

This is how it could unfold.

Monday Morning: The Spark

It begins quietly. Overnight, a report leaked that a major Asian economy—let's say China—has signed a landmark energy deal with Saudi Arabia. Oil contracts, once exclusively in dollars, will now be settled in yuan.

Markets stir uneasily. Commentators dismiss it as "symbolic." But traders smell blood. Futures spike. Currency desks twitch. The dollar dips 2% at the open. A tremor, nothing more.

By noon, social media explodes. Hashtags trend worldwide: #EndOfTheDollar. Memes circulate comparing the dollar to the Weimar mark. Influencers tell millions to "get out now."

Confidence—the fragile thread holding the empire together—begins to fray.

Tuesday: The Flight

By the second day, foreign central banks move. Russia and India announce they will diversify reserves away from the dollar. Brazil hints at the same. Bond markets convulse. U.S. Treasuries, once the "safest asset," are dumped in chunks. Yields skyrocket.

American politicians call for calm. The President assures citizens: "The dollar remains strong." The Fed issues a statement: "We stand ready to ensure stability."

But no words can halt panic once it takes hold. Corporations begin wiring funds abroad. Hedge funds scramble into gold and crypto. Ordinary Americans, watching their retirement accounts plunge, rush to withdraw cash. ATMs sputter. Apps freeze.

The flight has begun.

Wednesday: The Bank Runs

By midweek, the cracks widen into fractures. Regional banks face massive withdrawals. Digital transfers drain billions in hours. Regulators intervene, assuring deposits are "fully backed." But no one believes them.

Photos of long ATM lines spread online. Videos of angry crowds at locked bank doors go viral. Hashtags multiply: **#BankFail, #DollarCollapse.**

The illusion of safety evaporates. The bank run of the digital age is here— and it is national.

The Fed announces emergency liquidity injections. Trillions conjured. But printing is gasoline on the fire. Inflation expectations explode. The dollar plummets another 10%. Foreign exchange markets reel.

By evening, global headlines scream: **"The Dollar Crisis."**

Thursday: The Markets Shatter

Wall Street opens in freefall. Circuit breakers halt trading within minutes. Major corporations, dependent on cheap credit, watch their stock values evaporate. Pension funds collapse. Insurance companies wobble.

The derivatives bomb begins to tick. Margin calls ripple across institutions. A European megabank admits "liquidity challenges." Rumors swirl that a top U.S. investment bank is insolvent. Counterparties panic. Contracts fail.

This is no longer a currency crisis. It is a systemic collapse.

Friday: The Great Freeze

By the fifth day, governments move from persuasion to force.

The U.S. Treasury announces capital controls. Dollar transfers abroad are frozen. Banks impose withdrawal limits. Stock markets remain closed.

Citizens riot in major cities. Stores refuse to accept dollars, demanding alternative payments—gold, silver, crypto, foreign currency. Truckers halt deliveries, unwilling to take collapsing paper. Supply chains seize.

Abroad, allies distance themselves. Europe debates emergency adoption of a new "energy euro." BRICS nations declare a joint currency conference. China and Russia announce a new commodity-backed settlement system.

The empire is isolated. The illusion is dead.

Saturday and Sunday: The Silence

Over the weekend, the panic pauses—but not from relief. From exhaustion.

Banks remain shuttered. Supermarkets empty. Gas stations closed. Citizens huddle, fearful of what Monday will bring. Social media buzzes with speculation: Will the Fed print more? Will the military intervene? Will martial law be declared?

Foreign leaders convene emergency meetings. The G20 issues a vague statement of "stability." But behind the scenes, they prepare for a post-dollar world.

The silence is not calm. It is the breath before the plunge.

The New Monday: After the Dollar

When markets reopen, the dollar is no longer the dollar.

Its value has collapsed 50% in a week. Imports vanish. Inflation soars into double digits overnight. The empire's power to project strength abroad is gone. Aircraft carriers still float, but the fuel to run them must now be bought in currencies America no longer controls.

The Federal Reserve unveils a Central Bank Digital Currency, promising "stability" and "modernization." But citizens see it for what it is: surveillance and control. Millions reject it, turning instead to barter, crypto, gold, anything but fiat.

The illusion is over. The dollar has died—not in theory, not in prophecy, but in real time, in front of the world.

The Human Cost

Behind the headlines are lives shattered. Retirees lose savings. Families face skyrocketing prices for food and fuel. Businesses fail. Jobs vanish. The middle class, already fragile, is annihilated.

The empire that once promised endless prosperity collapses into scarcity. The dream is over. The reckoning is here.

And the tragedy is not that no one saw it coming. The tragedy is that millions did—but those in power chose denial over discipline, arrogance over reform, printing over prudence.

The day the dollar died will not be remembered for the charts, the markets, or the headlines. It will be remembered for the moment when billions realized, all at once, that the money they trusted was never real— that it was only faith, and faith is the most fragile currency of all.

CHAPTER 10

The Great Reset Reality

———————•———————

Every collapse invites a reconstruction. When chaos reigns, someone always steps forward with a blueprint for "order." The fall of Rome birthed feudal lords. The collapse of empires birthed colonies. The Great Depression birthed the New Deal.

So it will be when the dollar dies. The collapse will not end with empty shelves and bank runs. It will end with a proposal—a plan, polished and ready, waiting for the moment of panic to sell itself as salvation.

That plan has a name whispered in boardrooms, think tanks, and global summits: **The Great Reset.**

From Conspiracy to Policy

For years, "The Great Reset" was dismissed as conspiracy theory. A phrase coined by the World Economic Forum in 2020 during the pandemic, it was sold as a vague vision for sustainability and equity. Critics laughed. Politicians scoffed. The public shrugged.

But behind the buzzwords was something concrete: a framework for reorganizing the global economy once the old system failed. Debt forgiveness tied to digital currencies. Green initiatives tied to carbon credits. Universal IDs tied to financial access.

It wasn't a plan to prevent collapse. It was a plan to **manage the collapse.** And the dollar's death provides the perfect opening.

The Opportunity of Crisis

Never let a good crisis go to waste. This is the mantra of elites. And there is no greater crisis than the collapse of the world's reserve currency.

When millions are jobless, when savings are gone, when the streets are restless—people will accept any solution. And the Great Reset promises solutions. It offers digital stability, universal income, green recovery. But every solution carries a price: control.

The Great Reset is not about saving people. It is about saving power.

The Digital Dollar: Control in Disguise

At the center of the Reset is the **Central Bank Digital Currency (CBDC).** The Fed will unveil it as salvation after the collapse: "A new digital dollar to restore stability."

The pitch will be irresistible: no more bank runs, instant payments, guaranteed deposits. But hidden within is the end of financial freedom.

- **Programmable money:** Funds can be restricted for certain uses, expiring if not spent.

- **Total surveillance:** Every transaction tracked, every purchase logged.

- **Switchable access:** Accounts frozen with a keystroke for dissent, protest, or noncompliance.

This is the true Reset: not liberation, but digitized chains. The old dollar died of inflation and debt. The new dollar will live by obedience and control.

Debt Jubilee or Debt Trap?

The Reset will also promise debt forgiveness. Student loans wiped clean. Mortgages reduced. National debts "restructured." Citizens will cheer, believing they are free.

But freedom is an illusion. The forgiven debts will come with strings: acceptance of digital currency, compliance with carbon quotas, adherence to "social responsibility" scores. Refuse, and your relief evaporates.

The Reset does not erase chains. It replaces visible chains of debt with invisible chains of compliance.

Carbon Credits and Social Scores

The Great Reset intertwines finance with behavior. It does not simply ask what you buy—it asks why you buy.

Want to drive too often? Your carbon credits run out. Want to eat too much meat? Your "sustainability score" drops. Want to protest government policy? Your financial privileges pause.

This is not paranoia. Pilot programs already exist. China runs a social credit system. Europe experiments with carbon allowances. Corporations score consumers on "ESG compliance."

The Reset merely scales this globally, embedding it in the new digital currency. Money is no longer neutral—it becomes conditional.

The New Lords of Finance

In the Reset, sovereignty shifts. Not to elected governments, but to central banks, corporations, and supranational bodies.

The IMF, World Bank, and WEF present themselves as guardians of stability. In reality, they become unelected rulers. Nations desperate for relief surrender sovereignty for aid. Citizens desperate for survival surrender freedom for food.

The new lords of finance will not rule with armies but with algorithms.

Resistance and Division

But the Reset will not go unchallenged. Not everyone will comply. Gold hoarders, crypto advocates, black markets—they will resist. Communities will form parallel economies. Nations outside the globalist orbit will reject the digital leash.

The result will be division. A world split into two systems: the compliant bloc, digitized and controlled; and the dissident bloc, decentralized and defiant.

This conflict will define the post-dollar world. It will not be fought with bullets, but with currencies, trade agreements, and digital firewalls.

The Reality Beneath the Slogan

"The Great Reset" will be marketed with lofty slogans: Build Back Better. Green Recovery. Inclusive Capitalism.

But the reality is darker. It is the consolidation of power at the top, the reduction of freedom at the bottom, and the permanent severing of money from independence.

It is not about saving the planet. It is not about equity. It is about control.

The Harsh Truth

The Great Reset is not coming. It is already here—quietly prepared, quietly tested, quietly waiting. The collapse of the dollar is not just a tragedy. It is an opportunity for those who waited for chaos to seize the reins.

And when the Reset arrives, millions will welcome it. Not because they want it, but because they will be too desperate to refuse.

The Great Reset is not a conspiracy. It is a contingency plan. And when the dollar falls, it will become reality—not as salvation, but as the iron grip of control disguised as rescue.

CHAPTER 11

Life After Fiat

———————●———————

When the dollar dies, the world will not end. But the world we knew will.

Life after fiat is not an apocalypse, but transformation. A transformation as radical as the fall of Rome, as sudden as the Great Depression, as disruptive as the collapse of the Soviet Union. The empire may fall in a week, but the lives of ordinary people will change for decades.

The dollar's death will not simply mean new money. It will mean new rules, new behaviors, new ways of surviving. When faith in paper vanishes, people turn to the tangible, the trustworthy, the eternal.

Barter's Return

The first instinct in collapse is barter.

When currency no longer buys food, food becomes currency. A bag of rice is worth more than a stack of bills. A gallon of gas buys loyalty faster than a credit card. Tools, skills, and even favors become mediums of exchange.

This is not speculation—it is history. In Weimar Germany, farmers demanded shoes and tools in exchange for food. In Argentina's 2001 crisis, barter clubs flourished, swapping bread for medicine, labor for clothing. In Venezuela today, cigarettes and cans of tuna often trade more reliably than bolívars.

Life after fiat means the return of primitive exchange—not because people want it, but because necessity demands it.

Gold: The Ancient Refuge

When trust in governments dies, people reach for what has always endured: gold.

For 5,000 years, gold has been money. Empires rise and fall, paper comes and goes, but gold remains. It cannot be printed. It cannot be faked. It cannot be inflated away.

After the dollar's collapse, gold will return—not as a daily currency for buying groceries, but as the store of value behind serious transactions. Nations will settle debts in gold. Families will hoard coins and bars as protection against confiscation and hyperinflation. Black markets will price major goods in ounces, not bills.

The world will rediscover what it forgot: gold is not a "barbarous relic." It is survival.

Silver: The People's Metal

Gold protects wealth. Silver enables trade.

Historically, silver was the money of common people. Quarters, dimes, pesos, rupees—all once contained silver. After fiat's collapse, silver returns as the bridge between barter and gold. A few coins can buy food, fuel, or clothing. Small enough for daily use, valuable enough to store trust.

Silver is not just metal. It is liquidity for a world where paper burns.

Crypto: The Digital Escape

While metals return, a new contender rises: cryptocurrency.

Bitcoin, once mocked as a speculative toy, becomes a lifeline. Decentralized, borderless, resistant to censorship, it offers escape from collapsing fiat and predatory digital currencies imposed by governments.

In the aftermath, communities will transact peer-to-peer, bypassing banks and states. Stablecoins tied to commodities may emerge. Privacy coins shield citizens from surveillance. For the first time in history, people wield digital money not controlled by empires.

Crypto will not replace barter or metals. But it will carve a parallel world—an underground financial system where freedom survives.

Parallel Economies

Collapse creates division. Those who comply with the new digital system live under rules, surveillance, and rationing. Those who resist build parallel economies.

Farmers trade food directly. Craftsmen trade skills. Communities establish local scrip, backed by goods instead of government promises. Crypto networks flourish in the shadows.

Life after fiat is not uniform. It splits: the controlled economy of the Reset, and the free economy of the streets. Citizens will choose—or be forced—to navigate both.

Nations After Fiat

It is not only individuals who adapt. Nations too will find new paths.

- **Commodity-backed blocs:** BRICS nations, flush with resources, may anchor currencies to oil, gas, and metals.

- **Gold-backed trade:** Smaller states may stabilize themselves by pegging currencies to gold reserves.

- **Barter diplomacy:** Desperate nations may swap wheat for oil, lithium for grain, bypassing fiat entirely.

The world map will redraw itself not by ideology, but by resources. In life after fiat, sovereignty depends not on central banks but on what a nation can produce, mine, or harvest.

The New Middle Class: Producers, Not Consumers

The fiat era elevated consumers. Life after fiat elevates producers.

Those who make, grow, and repair will thrive. Farmers, mechanics, electricians, blacksmiths, coders, and doctors—skills become currency. Degrees lose value; abilities gain it.

The "middle class" of the new era is not defined by credit cards and mortgages. It is defined by usefulness.

Scarcity and Community

Collapse breeds scarcity. Scarcity breeds community.

As supply chains fracture, communities will turn inward. Local food networks, co-ops, and neighborhood defense groups will rise. Trust will shrink from nations to towns, from towns to families.

This is the paradox of life after fiat: the world becomes both more connected globally through barter and crypto—and more fragmented locally through survival networks.

The Shadow Markets

When governments impose digital currencies with restrictions, shadow markets will thrive. Already, in authoritarian states, underground economies rival official ones. In the post-dollar world, shadow markets will become lifelines.

Drugs, weapons, fuel, medicine—yes. But also food, clothing, and freedom. The Reset's digital leash will drive millions underground. And underground, the economy will live, resilient and defiant.

Lessons of the Past

History offers guidance:

- **Weimar Germany:** Those who held gold survived. Those who trusted paper perished.

- **Argentina 2001:** Barter clubs kept families alive.

- **Soviet collapse:** Black markets fed millions when official rations failed.

- **Venezuela:** Crypto adoption surged when bolívars became worthless.

Life after fiat is not a mystery. It is a cycle. And those who prepare for it will not only survive but thrive.

The Dawn After the Darkness

Life after fiat will be brutal, but it will not be eternal darkness. From the rubble, a new order will rise. People will rediscover resilience, independence, and the truth about value. Empires may dictate, but communities will endure.

The illusion of paper wealth will vanish. What remains is tangible, real, and eternal: food, family, skill, and trust.

When the dollar dies, life will not end. But the illusions will. And in their place, a harsher, more honest world will emerge—where money is not decreed from above but forged, earned, and trusted from below.

CHAPTER 12

The Road to Reconstruction

———————•———————

Every collapse is followed by reconstruction. Rubble becomes the foundation. Ashes become soil. Broken systems are replaced, not because people want change, but because they have no choice.

The fall of the dollar will be no different. When the illusions vanish, when fiat dies, when chaos burns through cities and markets, the survivors will begin the slow, painful work of rebuilding. The road to reconstruction is not paved with policies. It is carved through necessity, sacrifice, and grit.

And it will not begin in Washington. It will begin in the streets, the farms, the workshops, and the homes of those who refuse to die with the old system.

Stage One: Shock and Fragmentation

The first stage of reconstruction is not unity—it is fragmentation.

Communities pull inward. Towns, counties, and regions turn to local leadership as national authority collapses under mistrust. Police forces split between loyalty to government and loyalty to people. National Guard units protect some areas, abandon others.

The federal voice grows weaker. The local voice grows louder. Reconstruction begins not with grand plans, but with neighbors trading bread, bartering fuel, and forming defense groups.

It is raw, chaotic, and uneven. But it is the first step.

Stage Two: Parallel Structures

As the dust settles, parallel structures emerge.

- **Local currencies:** Communities print scripts, backed by goods or services. Farmers' cooperatives issue tokens redeemable for food. Towns accept silver coins, barter credits, or even crypto.

- **Mutual aid networks:** Churches, civic groups, and neighborhood councils step in where governments fail, organizing food distribution, water purification, and security patrols.

- **Alternative trade routes:** Truckers, once dependent on national supply chains, form private convoys between regions, trading goods outside the broken system.

These parallel structures are fragile, but they keep life moving. They are not official. They are not recognized. But they work—and they are trusted.

Stage Three: New Rules of Value

As communities stabilize, the old illusions of fiat are replaced by new rules of value.

- **Tangible > Abstract:** Land, tools, metals, and food are wealth. Paper is not.

- **Production > Consumption:** Those who create thrive. Those who only consume struggle.

- **Trust > Regulation:** Deals are enforced not by courts but by reputation. A man who cheats in barter is exiled. A community that honors contracts prospers.

Reconstruction is not just physical. It is moral. A new code of value emerges, forged by scarcity and necessity.

Stage Four: Regional Alliances

Over time, fragmented communities realize they cannot survive alone. Trade requires trust across distance. Defense requires coordination. Alliances form—regional compacts that pool resources, enforce basic rules, and create proto-governments.

These alliances may be pragmatic: farming regions trading with industrial zones, coastal ports supplying inland towns. They may be ideological: freedom-minded enclaves rejecting central control, collectivist regions embracing managed economies.

The United States does not vanish, but it fractures. The road to reconstruction is paved with competing visions.

Stage Five: National Reckoning

Eventually, a national reckoning arrives.

From the wreckage, new leadership emerges—whether military, populist, or technocratic. They promise unity, a return to strength, a new foundation. But this time, the illusion of fiat cannot return. Citizens will not trust paper again.

A new system must be built: commodity-backed currencies, digital trade tokens, or hybrid economies. The old model of infinite debt and printing is gone. The people demand something real.

This reckoning will be messy. It may involve conflict between regions, suppression of dissent, even civil war. But without it, the nation cannot move forward. Reconstruction requires not only survival—it requires rebirth.

Lessons from Other Collapses

History provides guidance for the road ahead:

- **Post-Soviet Russia (1990s):** Mafia groups filled the power vacuum. Black markets became lifelines. Eventually, a strong state reemerged, but freedom was sacrificed for stability.

- **Argentina (2001):** Local barter clubs sustained families until the peso stabilized. Citizens adapted, but trust in banks never returned.

- **Weimar Germany (1920s):** Hyperinflation destroyed savings. Reconstruction brought order—but also paved the way for authoritarianism.

These lessons are clear: reconstruction brings both opportunity and danger. Freedom can be reborn, or tyranny can rise from desperation.

The Role of Technology

Unlike past collapses, this one unfolds in the digital age.

- **Crypto networks** will allow resistant communities to bypass government control, creating digital barter zones across borders.

- **Surveillance tech** will empower governments to impose digital currencies with conditions.

- **Decentralized tools**—3D printers, solar panels, satellite internet—will give individuals unprecedented resilience.

Technology is a double-edged sword. It can empower freedom or cement tyranny. Reconstruction will be shaped by who wields it.

The Individual's Road

For individuals, the road to reconstruction is both external and internal.

Externally, it means learning to survive: growing food, securing water, protecting family, building networks. Internally, it means shedding illusions: realizing that wealth is not digits on a screen, that freedom is not granted by governments, that survival requires adaptation.

The road is harsh. But those who embrace reality instead of longing for the past will thrive.

The Glimmer of Renewal

Collapse destroys illusions. But it also clears the ground for renewal.

Communities rediscover independence. Families rediscover resilience. Nations rediscover what money truly is. The reconstruction may be brutal, but it is also a chance—a chance to rebuild on truth rather than deception.

The empire that dies may give birth to something more honest, more grounded, more enduring. If—and only if—the people choose wisely.

The road to reconstruction will not be paved with easy answers or painless solutions. It will be carved in hardship, tested by conflict, and lit by the faint but enduring flame of human resilience. From the ashes of fiat, a new world will rise—but whether it is freer or more enslaved depends on the choices made in the crucible of collapse.

CHAPTER 13

Board-Supervised Family Notifications for the ID Switch

———————•———————

Collapse is not only about money. It is about identity.

When the dollar dies, when the old system fractures, governments and institutions will not only rebuild currencies—they will rebuild citizens. And that process begins with identification. Who are you? What do you own? What do you owe? What do you deserve?

The new order will not take your word for it. It will demand proof. It will demand compliance. And it will demand that your identity—the one tied to collapsing fiat, old debts, old freedoms—be switched to a new one, bound to the Great Reset.

That process will be messy. Families will be pulled into bureaucratic battles. Oversight boards will be created to enforce compliance. And citizens, stripped of choice, will be notified not as free individuals, but as dependents under supervision.

This is the ID switch.

The Birth of the Oversight Boards

When chaos erupts, governments move quickly to consolidate control. Amid bank failures and riots, special **Reconstruction Oversight Boards** are formed. On paper, they promise to "restore order." In reality, they become arbiters of identity.

The boards are tasked with "supervising family notifications" of the transition to digital ID. Their mission: ensure every citizen is registered into the new system, every family notified of obligations, every dissent tracked.

It sounds clinical. It is invasive.

Imagine a faceless committee, staffed by bureaucrats, corporate consultants, and technocrats, deciding not just how money flows but how lives are redefined. Their memos become law. Their notifications dictate survival.

The ID Switch Process

The ID switch is marketed as modernization: *"A unified digital ID for efficiency, safety, and equality."* But the reality is stark.

1. **Family Notifications:** Households receive official notices—letters, emails, text messages—stating that existing IDs, bank accounts, and benefits will expire unless switched to the new system.

2. **Compliance Deadlines:** Families are given fixed windows to present themselves at registration centers or risk losing access to food, healthcare, and financial services.

3. **Biometric Enrollment:** The new ID requires fingerprints, retinal scans, voice prints. The system ties your body to your account.

4. **Debt and Asset Integration:** Old debts are reviewed, consolidated, and reattached to your new identity. Assets are logged, sometimes seized, sometimes reduced.

5. **Conditional Access:** Benefits are tied to behavior. Compliance ensures privileges. Resistance ensures exclusion.

The switch is not optional. It is survival.

Families in Crisis

For families, the notifications become moments of fracture. Parents argue over compliance. Children demand answers. Grandparents, distrustful of technology, resist.

- In one home, a father tells his family they must comply: *"We can't afford to lose access to food."*

- In another, a mother refuses, hiding her children's biometric data: *"We survived the collapse—we won't bow now."*

- In yet another, siblings fight over whether to trade family silver for exemptions, tearing generations apart.

The ID switch is not just administrative. It is personal. It reshapes families as much as economies.

The Burden of Notifications

Oversight boards know the power of fear. Notifications are worded to terrify:

"Failure to enroll will result in suspension of benefits."
"Household noncompliance will trigger investigation."
"Children under 18 must be enrolled by guardians within 30 days."

Families open envelopes and feel their hearts sink. A simple letter becomes a threat: comply or starve.

Even compliant families live in fear. What if the system glitches? What if their notification is delayed? What if a bureaucrat misfiles their enrollment? Survival hangs not on freedom but on paperwork.

The Disputes and the Hearings

Inevitably, disputes erupt. Some families contest debts attached to their new IDs. Others argue over property ownership. Some demand exemptions on religious or moral grounds.

The boards respond with hearings. Families sit before panels of strangers who decide their fate.

- One family argues their deceased father's debt should not carry forward. The board rules otherwise.

- Another protests biometric enrollment for children. The board denies the request, labeling them "noncompliant."

- A widow begs to keep her savings outside the system. The board confiscates it, citing "national stability."

The hearings are not justice. They are ritualized humiliation. Citizens plead for dignity. Boards issue decrees. And the system grinds forward.

The Black Markets of Identity

Not everyone complies. Resistance breeds alternatives.

In underground markets, forged IDs appear. Hackers offer "parallel profiles" untethered from board oversight. Communities create shadow registries, barter-based and trust-driven. Parents enroll children officially but maintain secret aliases in hidden networks.

The black markets are dangerous—punishable by imprisonment. But for many, they are the only way to preserve autonomy. The ID switch does not erase resistance. It multiplies it.

Psychological Fallout

The ID switch is more than bureaucracy. It is a trauma.

Families lose the illusion of privacy. Children grow up knowing their identities are tracked, their choices scored. Parents feel powerless, reduced to functionaries of the system. Trust between generations erodes—those who comply resent those who resist; those who resist despise those who submit.

The collapse fractured the economy. The ID switch fractures the soul.

The Broader Implications

The ID switch is not just about families. It is about control on a civilizational scale.

- **Governments** use IDs to enforce compliance with new currencies, taxes, and quotas.

- **Corporations** use IDs to filter customers: only the "approved" may buy, sell, or work.

- **Global bodies** use IDs to manage migration, trade, and aid distribution.

Identity becomes currency. Without the right ID, you do not exist.

The Illusion of Choice

Politicians insist: *"Participation is voluntary."* But the choice is false.

Refuse the ID, and you lose access to healthcare. Refuse, and your children cannot attend school. Refuse, and you are cut off from digital currency. Refuse, and you become an outlaw in your own land.

The road to reconstruction, it turns out, is paved not with freedom but with conditional survival. Families are not rebuilding their lives—they are surrendering them.

The board-supervised family notifications for the ID switch will not be remembered as bureaucratic routine. They will be remembered as the moment when millions realized they had not survived collapse to regain freedom, but to trade one illusion for another—paper money for digital chains, debt for compliance, liberty for survival.

CHAPTER 14

Open Books Day — Trust Corrections and Disclosure Tested

—————•—————

In every collapse, there comes a moment when the rulers, desperate to restore faith, demand transparency. Not real transparency, not the kind that empowers citizens—but staged transparency. Managed openness. A controlled ritual of disclosure designed to pacify a restless public.

After the ID switch rolled out, after families were notified and supervised, the new Reconstruction Oversight Boards announced their next initiative: **Open Books Day.**

It was marketed as a day of truth. A day where records would be opened, accounts reconciled, and trust restored. But in practice, it was a day of exposure and humiliation, a test not of honesty but of obedience.

The Announcement

The decree spread everywhere at once:

"On Open Books Day, all citizens are required to present their financial, personal, and social records for verification. The purpose is to correct discrepancies, rebuild trust, and ensure fairness in the new economy."

The slogan was simple: **"Trust Through Transparency."**

Posters appeared on street corners. Broadcasts repeated it hourly. Social media flooded with propaganda: families smiling as they shared their "open books," children waving new digital IDs, slogans promising a brighter tomorrow.

But behind the marketing was a warning: *"Failure to participate will result in suspension of digital access and review by the Board."*

It wasn't a suggestion. It was a command.

The Mechanics of Disclosure

On Open Books Day, families were summoned to designated centers—schools, courthouses, auditoriums converted into registration halls. Each household was assigned a time slot. Each was told to bring documentation: property records, debt histories, medical records, proof of compliance with prior ID notifications.

At the centers, officials sat at long tables with screens and scanners. Families were ushered forward one by one. Data was cross-checked. Inconsistencies flagged. Questions asked.

The process felt less like reconciliation and more like interrogation.

- A farmer was told his land was misclassified. He protested, but his appeal was denied. His land was reassigned to "national agricultural use."

- A widow was told her savings exceeded her declared income. She insisted it was inheritance. Officials froze half her account pending "review."

- A young mother was told her child's enrollment was incomplete. She argued the paperwork had been filed. Officials threatened suspension of her family's benefits.

The corrections were not about accuracy. They were about control.

The Spectacle of Compliance

Open Books Day was designed as a public ritual. Families lined up in visible queues. Screens projected compliance rates in real time: *"District 7: 92% Complete."* News outlets broadcast live footage, praising the "spirit of cooperation."

But the spectacle cut both ways. Citizens saw neighbors reprimanded in public, their errors announced, their privileges suspended. Rumors spread of "noncompliant" households disappearing after disclosure. Fear seeped into every corner of the ritual.

Compliance became performance. Citizens smiled, nodded, and thanked officials, even as they seethed inside.

The Test of Trust

The Boards framed Open Books Day as a test of trust. Citizens were told: *"If you have nothing to hide, you have nothing to fear."*

But everyone had something to fear.

For some, it was undeclared assets—silver coins, hidden crypto wallets, barter arrangements. For others, it was debts carried forward unfairly, mistakes in records, or bureaucratic errors. For many, it was simply the fear that any discrepancy, no matter how small, could be interpreted as defiance.

Trust, in reality, was one-sided. The people opened their lives. The Boards offered nothing in return. The ledgers of corporations, the accounts of elites, the dealings of the powerful remained closed.

The slogan should have read: **"Trust Us. You, however, will be tested."**

Resistance and Exposure

Not everyone complied.

Some families refused to attend. Others showed up but presented incomplete records. A few tried to falsify documents or hide assets.

The Boards responded with ruthless efficiency. Names of "noncompliant" households were published publicly. Digital access was cut off. Benefits suspended. In extreme cases, families were relocated to "trust review centers."

The message was clear: disclosure was not about fairness. It was about submission.

And yet resistance grew. Underground networks advised families on how to withhold information. Communities developed "dual books"—one for officials, one for survival. Hackers disrupted data uploads, erasing records mid-process.

The more the Boards demanded disclosure, the more citizens learned to conceal.

The Collapse of Illusion

By the end of Open Books Day, officials declared victory: *"98% compliance achieved. Trust restored. Transparency is successful."*

But the victory was hollow.

Citizens walked away humiliated, distrustful, angrier than before. They saw neighbors punished arbitrarily. They saw the double standard: the poor exposed, the powerful untouched. They realized that "Open Books" was not about truth. It was about control.

The Boards believed they had tested disclosure. In reality, disclosure had tested them—and they had failed.

Trust cannot be manufactured. It cannot be enforced by notifications, hearings, or disclosures. It must be earned. And in the crucible of collapse, the Boards revealed not honesty but tyranny.

The Personal Fallout

For families, the fallout was devastating.

- Parents warned children never to speak openly about hidden assets.

- Spouses argued over compliance versus concealment, trust versus survival.

- Communities fractured between those who obeyed and those who resisted.

The collapse had already eroded wealth. Now Open Books Day eroded trust—not just in government, but within families, neighborhoods, and friends.

The illusion of transparency had destroyed the very thing it claimed to rebuild.

Open Books Day will be remembered not as the rebirth of trust, but as its funeral. A day when citizens learned that disclosure under threat is not honesty—it is submission. And submission cannot rebuild what collapse destroyed.

CHAPTER 15

Town Forum and Vigil
— The Policy of Transparency Meets the
Anger of the People

———————•———————

Collapse does not end quietly. It festers, it smolders, and then, when pressed too hard, it erupts.

The Boards believed they could pacify the nation with rituals of compliance. ID switches. Open Books Day. Family notifications. But every decree carved resentment deeper. Every humiliation lit another fuse. And when they summoned the people to a town forum to "explain transparency," they did not invite peace. They invited fire.

The Gathering

It was a gray evening when the forum began. The local auditorium, once a school gym, was converted into a stage for the Oversight Board's representatives. Banners hung on the walls: **"Transparency Builds Trust. Trust Builds Tomorrow."**

Rows of plastic chairs filled with families—mothers, fathers, children clutching hands. Farmers in dusty boots. Nurses in faded uniforms. Pensioners with weary eyes. They came because attendance was mandatory.

At the front sat the Board delegation—suits, tablets, prepared smiles. They had come not to listen, but to lecture. To "explain policy." To assure the public that everything was under control.

But the faces in the crowd told another story: anger, suspicion, grief.

The Opening Words

The lead representative rose, microphone in hand. His voice was steady, rehearsed.

"Citizens, we understand your concerns. Open Books Day was not punishment—it was fairness. We must all share the burden to rebuild. Transparency is the cornerstone of trust. Without it, there can be no reconstruction."

The words echoed in the hall. But instead of applause, silence thickened. Then came a murmur. Then a voice.

"What about the banks that never opened their books?" a man shouted. *"Why are we the only ones exposed?"*

Applause erupted. Others joined in. *"Where's the disclosure from the corporations? From the politicians? From you?"*

The representative faltered. The slogans on the wall suddenly looked like accusations.

The Anger Unleashed

Questions became accusations. Accusations became shouts.

- A mother demanded to know why her family's benefits were cut after a clerical error.

- A farmer accused the Board of seizing his land under false pretenses.

- A pensioner sobbed that his life savings had been "corrected" into nothing.

Every grievance was a wound, and the wounds were countless. The hall became a storm of voices, the air electric with rage.

The representatives tried to calm the crowd. They spoke of unity, of rebuilding, of sacrifice. But their words were drowned in jeers. The people had come to listen. They left shouting.

The Vigil Begins

When the forum ended in chaos, the crowd did not disperse. They spilled into the town square, carrying candles. Some had brought them in silent preparation. Others lit phones and lanterns.

What began as a protest became vigil.

Names were read aloud: neighbors who had lost homes, families who had been cut off, elders who had died waiting for medical access. Each name was followed by silence, then murmurs of *"never again."*

The vigil was not organized. It was spontaneous. But it carried more power than the forum's stage-managed slogans. For the first time, grief and anger fused into solidarity.

The Clash of Symbols

In the square, the Board's banners still fluttered: **"Transparency Builds Trust."** Citizens tore them down. They replaced them with hand-painted signs:

"We Trusted, You Stole."
"Transparency For All—Not Just Us."
"No More Chains."

Candles burned at the base of the torn banners, symbols of mourning turned into defiance.

For the Boards, transparency was a tool of control. For the people, transparency became a demand for justice.

The Turning Point

As night deepened, the vigil grew. Hundreds, then thousands gathered. Word spread through nearby towns. Videos went viral despite censors. The square glowed with firelight and chants.

The Boards, watching from behind guarded walls, debated their response. Some urged a crackdown. Others urged appeasement. But the truth was clear: the policy of forced transparency had backfired.

The people no longer feared exposure. They demanded it—from those who ruled.

The Human Element

In the crowd, families held each other. Strangers shared food and water. A priest led a prayer. A nurse sang softly. Children drew chalk outlines of keys and locks on the pavement, symbols of freedom long lost.

It was not just a protest. It was a community reclaiming its voice.

For months, citizens had been divided by compliance and resistance. The forum, meant to deepen division, had done the opposite. It had given the people a common enemy: hypocrisy.

The Breaking of Illusions

The vigil marked a breaking point.

- The illusion that transparency was fairness was shattered.

- The illusion that obedience restored trust was exposed as a lie.

- The illusion that the Boards held unshakable power was cracked.

For the first time since the collapse, the people realized they were not powerless. There were many. The Boards were few.

The Foreshadowing of Fire

No violence erupted that night. The candles burned peacefully. The chants echoed but no stones were thrown.

But beneath the calm, fire smoldered.

The people had seen the mask slip. They had felt their collective strength. The Boards could still threaten, still punish, still control—but the illusion of legitimacy was gone.

And once legitimacy dies, power crumbles.

The town forum was meant to explain policy. The vigil was meant to mourn loss. But together, they became something greater: the moment when anger turned into unity, when grief turned into defiance, when the policy of transparency collapsed under the weight of its own hypocrisy.

CHAPTER 16

The TRO Hearing — Access Roads, Testimonies, and Temporary Resistance

———————•———————

Collapse always bleeds into the courts. When the streets erupt, when the squares glow with vigil fires, when families defy the Boards, governments turn to law as their shield. Not true justice. Not impartial rule. But law as a weapon.

And so it was after the forum and vigil. The Boards, rattled by the display of unity, sought to cut off dissent before it spread. Their method was surgical: choke the lifelines. Block the access roads that led to gathering sites. Control the flow of goods, people, and information.

The people responded with the only tool left within the system: a petition for a **Temporary Restraining Order (TRO)**. A desperate plea to the courts to stop the closures, if only for a time.

The TRO hearing became more than a legal proceeding. It became a battlefield.

The Access Roads

The access roads were more than asphalt. They were arteries of survival.

They carried food from rural farms to urban markets. They carried fuel from depots to towns. They carried families from one community to another. They carried the very spirit of resistance from isolated pockets into united movements.

When the Boards moved to close them, citing "safety concerns" after the vigil, it was clear what they intended: suffocate the movement before it grew. Cut off the people from one another.

But the closures were not absolute. Some trucks still slipped through. Some convoys defied orders. And now the people sought to pry open those roads legally, even temporarily.

The Courtroom as Theater

On the morning of the hearing, the courthouse was surrounded. Farmers in boots. Nurses in scrubs. Families carrying signs:

"Our Roads, Our Lives."
"Transparency Without Access Is Tyranny."

Inside, the air was thick with tension. Judges in black robes sat like statues. Lawyers shuffled papers. Board representatives whispered behind their masks of composure.

The hearing was about law. But everyone knew it was also about legitimacy. Could the people bend the system back against its masters, if only for a moment?

The Testimonies

One by one, citizens testified.

- A farmer spoke of rotting crops he could not deliver because the road to the market was blocked.

- A mother described her child's medical emergency, the ambulance delayed by barricades.

- A trucker told of convoys harassed by Board patrols, food confiscated under "compliance inspections."

Their voices cracked with desperation, but they did not falter. Each testimony was a blade cutting through the illusion that road closures were about safety. The truth was naked: they were about control.

When the Board's lawyer rose, his words were precise, polished, soulless: *"The closures are temporary measures to prevent escalation of unrest. The public interest requires stability."*

The room hissed with anger. Stability, the people thought, for whom?

The Clash of Narratives

The people argued about survival. The Boards argued order.

The judge, caught between them, played the role of neutrality. But neutrality itself was an illusion. Everyone knew the courts had long been an arm of the system. And yet, even in collapse, the ritual mattered. The hearing mattered. Because it gave the people a stage, a microphone, a record.

And sometimes, even regimes must bow—if only to buy time.

The Temporary Resistance

After hours of arguments, after testimonies that painted suffering in raw detail, the judge delivered the ruling:

"The closures of access roads are hereby suspended for thirty days, pending further review. During this period, the Boards may enforce safety inspections but may not obstruct essential travel."

The room erupted. Cheers mixed with tears. It was not a victory. It was reprieve. Thirty days of breathing room. Thirty days of connection. Thirty days of life.

The Boards bristled. Their lawyers filed appeals instantly. But the people had won a sliver of resistance, a wedge of space carved out by law itself.

The Symbol Beyond the Ruling

The TRO was more than paper. It became a symbol.

Communities reopened convoys, escorted by crowds waving flags. Farmers delivered food in celebratory processions. Truckers honked horns in defiance.

The victory was fragile, temporary, conditional—but it was victory nonetheless. And in collapse, victories were rare.

For the people, the ruling proved something vital: the system could be forced to bend, however slightly. Resistance was not futile.

The Fragility of Hope

Yet hope was fragile. Everyone knew the Boards would return stronger, more ruthless. Everyone knew the reprieve was short. Thirty days could pass in a blink.

But for thirty days, resistance had room to breathe. For thirty days, families could reconnect. For thirty days, the fire of unity burned brighter.

And in those thirty days, the people prepared—not for compliance, but for confrontation.

The TRO hearing did not overturn the system. It did not topple the Boards. But it gave the people something more dangerous than victory: hope. And in the ruins of collapse, hope is the spark that regimes fear most.

CHAPTER 17

Testimonies of the Trustee
— Truth Against the Machine

———————•———————

Every system in collapse creates its scapegoats—and its witnesses. When corruption festers, when tyranny hides behind procedure, someone eventually steps forward to speak truth. That person becomes both a weapon and target.

In the aftermath of the TRO victory, the Boards convened another hearing. This time, not about roads or benefits, but about compliance at the highest level. The stage was set not for farmers or truckers, but for the **Trustee**—a figure appointed to oversee reconstruction, chosen to symbolize neutrality, burdened with the impossible role of restoring legitimacy.

The Trustee was supposed to be a caretaker of records, an enforcer of rules, a steward of order. But when summoned to testify, the Trustee broke the script.

And in doing so, truth slammed headfirst into the machine.

The Chamber of Authority

The hearing chamber was grander than the TRO courtroom. Flags lined the walls. Cameras streamed live across the nation. Citizens were told this was a "public inquiry" into the Trustee's conduct, a test of accountability.

But everyone knew the real purpose: intimidation. The Boards wanted a display of dominance. They wanted the Trustee to bow, to affirm their legitimacy. They wanted the nation to see compliance from the very figure meant to represent integrity.

Instead, they got defiance.

The Oath

The Trustee rose, hand raised, eyes steady. The oath was recited: *"Do you swear to speak the truth, the whole truth, nothing but the truth?"*

A pause. Then: *"I swear. And I will not recite half-truths for your comfort."*

A murmur rippled through the chamber. The words were small, but the defiance was clear. The Trustee had stepped out of their role as custodian—and into the role of witness.

The First Questions

The questioning began predictably.

"Trustee, do you affirm that Open Books Day achieved transparency?"
"No," the Trustee replied. *"It achieved exposure of the weak and concealment of the powerful."*

"Do you affirm that the ID switch improved compliance?"
"No. It fractured families, destroyed trust, and gave you control at the expense of unity."

Each answer was sharper than the last, slicing through the carefully scripted narrative. Board members shifted in their seats, their smiles frozen, their fury restrained by cameras.

The People's Witness

As the testimony continued, the Trustee became the people's voice.

- They recounted families humiliated in hearings.

- They described the vigil, not as "unrest," but as mourning turned to unity.

- They named the hypocrisy of officials who demanded disclosure from citizens while hiding their own accounts offshore.

Every word was a spark. And outside the chamber, crowds gathered around screens, listening, cheering quietly, tears running down faces. For the first time, truth was spoken in the machine's own house.

The Machine Strikes Back

But truth is dangerous. The Board's lead examiner leaned forward, voice sharp:

"Trustee, do you admit your testimony undermines stability?"
"I admit it undermines lies."

"Do you understand that false statements here are punishable by removal?"
"Then remove me. Better removed for truth than honored for silence."

The chamber gasped. Officials whispered furiously. The cameras kept rolling.

The Trustee had not just testified—they had declared war.

The Turning of the Crowd

The people watching sensed the shift. In markets, in squares, in homes lit by candlelight, citizens leaned closer to screens. The Trustee's words echoed their own anger, their own grief, their own longing for honesty.

For months, the Boards had claimed to represent order. But in a single testimony, the Trustee revealed the opposite: the Boards represented control, while the people represented truth.

The hearing, meant to be a display of authority, became a broadcast of rebellion.

The Closing Statement

As questioning ended, the Trustee was allowed a final statement. They did not hesitate.

"This system calls itself reconstruction. But it is not reconstruction—it is domination. You claim transparency, but you fear disclosure of your own corruption. You claim compliance, but you have destroyed unity. You claim stability, but you have created desperation. If this machine continues, it will collapse under its own weight. And when it does, it will not be me you fear—it will be the people you betrayed."

The words struck like thunder. Silence followed, then hurried adjournment. Officials scrambled to shut down the feed. But it was too late. The testimony had been heard.

Aftermath

That night, the Trustee was escorted under guard. Rumors swirled—removal, arrest, exile. The Boards insisted the testimony was "reckless." But the people did not see recklessness. They saw courage.

In towns and villages, candles were lit again, not for mourning, but for defiance. The Trustee had spoken truth against the machine, and in doing so, they had ignited hope.

The system had tried to weaponize law to silence dissent. Instead, law became the stage where dissent found its loudest voice.

The testimonies of the Trustee will be remembered not as evidence in a case, but as prophecy in a trial—a moment when truth pierced the machine, and the people realized the system could no longer command their faith.

CHAPTER 18

The TRO Extension
— Thirty More Days of Fire

———————•———————

In collapse, time is currency. A day without oppression is wealth. A week of breathing space is luxury. A month of reprieve is revolution.

When the judge granted the first TRO—thirty days to keep the access roads open—the people treated it as a miracle. When the Boards appealed, they expected it overturned. But when the court, under pressure from testimony, public outrage, and the Trustee's words, extended the TRO for another thirty days, the people erupted.

It was not just thirty days of access. It was thirty days of fire.

The Announcement

The ruling came quietly, buried in legal filings. But word spread like wildfire. Screens lit up with headlines:

"TRO EXTENDED: Access Roads Remain Open for Thirty More Days."

Crowds cheered in markets. Truckers blared horns in defiance. Farmers raised fists in fields. Nurses in clinics wept with relief. The extension meant food, medicine, fuel, and connection would flow for another month.

But it meant more than survival. It meant momentum.

The Shift in Spirit

The first TRO had been met with cautious relief. The people were grateful but wary, knowing the reprieve was fragile.

The extension, however, felt different. It was not just survival—it was validation. It proved that resistance was working. That the Boards, despite their power, could be forced to bend. That unity mattered.

The people's posture shifted. They no longer begged. They demanded. They no longer whispered. They roared.

Thirty Days of Defiance

In those thirty days, life surged.

- **Convoys returned to the roads,** no longer sneaking under cover of night but moving in daylight, escorted by crowds who lined highways, waving banners and chanting slogans.

- **Markets flourished,** with barter and silver flowing openly, guarded by volunteers who stood watch against raids.

- **Assemblies gathered,** no longer just vigils but open councils where citizens debated strategies, planned defenses, and coordinated aid.

The reprieve had become a staging ground. The thirty days were not idle—they were preparation.

The Anger of the Boards

The Boards seethed. To them, the TRO extension was humiliation. Their power had been challenged in court, their legitimacy shattered in testimony, their authority mocked in streets.

They responded with warnings: *"Noncompliance will not be tolerated after the TRO expires."*
They deployed more patrols, drones, and checkpoints around cities. They tightened surveillance.

But the harder they squeezed, the more the people slipped through. The fire was spreading too fast.

The Trustee's Shadow

Though silenced, possibly imprisoned, the Trustee's testimony echoed. Quotes circulated like scripture: *"Better removed for truth than honored for silence."*

Murals appeared on walls, painting the Trustee as a figure of defiance. Children scrawled their name in chalk. Families repeated their words around fires at night.

The Boards had tried to bury the Trustee. Instead, they had created a martyr of truth.

And with the TRO extension, the people believed they were fighting in the Trustee's shadow.

Thirty Days of Fire

The extension unleashed a wave of action.

- **Protests swelled,** filling streets in major towns, candles in one hand, placards in the other.

- **Songs emerged,** chanted in crowds, hummed in homes, carrying messages of defiance: "Thirty Days of Fire, Thirty Days of Light."

- **Networks grew,** as communities once divided by fear now linked across reopened roads, forming coalitions too broad to silence.

Every day became another spark. Every night became another vigil. The Boards had hoped the reprieve would calm the people. Instead, it gave them time to organize.

The Fragility of Power

The extension revealed something the Boards feared: their power was fragile.

For months, they had ruled through fear and decrees. But when faced with resistance backed by law and fueled by unity, their dominance faltered. The machine was not invincible.

The people realized it too. They had thirty days not to wait, but to prepare for what came next.

Preparing for the Endgame

As the days passed, whispers spread: *"What happens when the thirty days end?"*

Some urged negotiation. Others urged escalation. Many believed the Boards would strike hard, crushing resistance with overwhelming force once the TRO expired.

But the people were no longer unprepared. They stockpiled supplies, fortified routes, and trained volunteers. They mapped shadow networks for barter and communication. They turned thirty days into a launchpad for survival beyond law.

The Boards thought the extension was a leash. The people made it a weapon.

The TRO extension was not a pause in the fire. It was the fire itself—thirty days of defiance, thirty days of unity, thirty days where the people learned that power was not permanent, and fear was not destiny. Thirty days that lit the fuse for what came next.

CHAPTER 19

The Great Disclosure Breach
— Leaks, Secrets, and Collapse of Control

———————•———————

Power survives through secrecy. The Boards had ruled by demanding disclosure from the people while guarding their own records in fortified vaults, encrypted servers, and hidden accounts. They told citizens, *"Open your books,"* but never opened theirs.

That illusion ended the night of the breach.

The Great Disclosure Breach was not planned by governments or institutions. It was sparked in shadows—by hackers, whistleblowers, and insiders who had seen too much. When it broke, it tore through the empire's last veil of legitimacy. The machine of control, built on fear and deception, collapsed under its own hidden truths.

The First Leak

It began with a file—anonymous, unsigned, dumped into public forums at midnight.

The document was a spreadsheet, stamped with the Board's seal. It listed accounts: offshore banks, hidden reserves, assets quietly transferred while citizens were forced to surrender theirs.

At first, few believed it. But within hours, confirmations poured in. Account numbers matched. Signatures aligned. Journalists, though censored, whispered that the leak was authentic.

The hypocrisy was naked. While families lost homes for "corrections," Board members had siphoned billions into untouchable vaults.

The first leak was a spark. The firestorm followed.

The Breach Unleashed

Within days, more files spilled. Emails detailing secret meetings with corporations. Video recordings of closed-door sessions where Board officials mocked citizens as "useful cattle." Internal memos proving Open Books Day was never about trust but about surveillance quotas.

Encrypted servers, thought untouchable, were cracked open. Data flooded into the public domain faster than censors could block it. Screens lit up across towns and cities with damning evidence.

What the people had long suspected was no longer a rumor. It was true, raw and undeniable.

The Collapse of Narrative

For months, the Boards had controlled the story. They were the guardians of order, the stewards of reconstruction. Their slogans were repeated endlessly: *"Transparency Builds Trust."*

But the leaks inverted the narrative. Now every slogan was mocked. Memes spread showing smiling officials under banners: *"Transparency for You, Secrecy for Us."*

The public no longer debated whether the Boards were corrupt. They debated how long before they fell.

Secrets of the Machine

Among the most explosive revelations were the "compliance algorithms." Documents showed that every citizen had been scored—not just for finances, but for behavior, beliefs, even associations. Families had been punished not for mistakes, but for being flagged as "noncompliant risks."

Worse still were the medical files. Evidence showed experimental surveillance implants proposed for future IDs. Plans to tie carbon credits not just to purchases but to biometric data.

The breach did not reveal policies. It revealed blueprints for total control.

The machine had been exposed in full—and it terrified even those who once obeyed it.

The People's Reaction

The reaction was volcanic.

Crowds filled the squares again, this time not in vigil but in fury. Citizens carried banners not of plea but of accusation:

"You Lied."
"Your Books Are Open Now."
"No Forgiveness."

Protests swelled into blockades. Roads once controlled by Boards were seized by convoys of farmers and truckers. Markets refused digital IDs, openly trading in silver and barter.

The leaks had not just broken trust—they had dissolved obedience.

The Boards in Panic

Inside their towers, the Boards scrambled. Emergency meetings stretched through nights. Statements were drafted: *"The leaks are forgeries."* But denials rang hollow—too much proof, too many confirmations.

Some officials fled. Others doubled down, demanding censorship, arrests, and harsher measures. But the machine was cracking from within.

Whistleblowers multiplied. Insiders, seeing collapse inevitable, leaked even more. Officials turned on one another, desperate to shift blame.

The machine was eating itself.

The Great Disclosure

By the end of the breach, the entire archive of Board documents had been dumped online. Citizens scrolled through thousands of pages: secret deals, asset transfers, surveillance programs, plans for indefinite emergency rule.

It became known as the **Great Disclosure.** Not because the Boards intended it, but because truth, once buried, had erupted uncontrollably.

For the first time in years, the people had more information than the rulers. Power shifted—not officially, not legally, but psychologically. The illusion of control was gone.

Collapse of Control

The consequences were immediate.

- **Cities erupted,** with entire districts declaring themselves autonomous from the Boards.

- **Board patrols were defied,** sometimes peacefully, sometimes violently.

- **Markets split,** half still under surveillance, half fully underground.

- **Officials disappeared,** hunted not by assassins but by their own guilt and fear.

The Boards had survived protests, vigils, and courts. But they could not survive their own secrets. The breach had turned the machine inside out.

Control had collapsed.

The Human Cost of Truth

But the truth is not gentle.

Families discovered their neighbors had been informants. Friends learned their names were flagged in compliance reports. Betrayals surfaced, not imagined but documented.

The Great Disclosure freed the people from illusions—but it also poisoned trust at the most personal level. Communities fractured, not just against the Boards, but against one another.

Truth liberated. Truth also burned.

The Great Disclosure Breach will be remembered as the moment the machine bled out—not by bullets or fire, but by its own hidden truths spilling into the light. Secrets meant to bind power became the knife that severed it, and with their collapse, the people stepped into a world where lies no longer ruled—but where trust itself lay in ashes.

CHAPTER 20

The Vigil of Resolve
— From Ashes to the Next Morning

————————•————————

The empire had fallen into its own contradictions. The dollar was gone. The Boards, once invincible, staggered under the weight of exposure. Secrets had spilled, trust had burned, and obedience had collapsed.

Yet collapse is never the end. It is the moment before choice. The people, stripped of illusions, now faced the question: what comes next?

That night, they gathered again—not in anger, not in mourning alone, but in resolve. It was called the **Vigil of Resolve.**

The Gathering

The square, once the scene of protests and forums, filled once more. Families carried candles, torches, lanterns, anything that gave light in the darkness of power outages.

There were no banners this time, no slogans pre-written. Instead, signs scrawled in chalk and charcoal read:

"No More Lies."
"Truth Is Our Currency."
"Never Again."

Children clutched their parents' hands. Elders sat in wheelchairs, wrapped in blankets. Farmers came with dust still on their boots. Truckers rolled in and parked their rigs as barricades. Nurses arrived straight from clinics. The vigil was not organized. It was organic.

It was not a protest. It was a pledge.

The Silence

Unlike the fiery chants of earlier demonstrations, the vigil began in silence. The crowd stood still as names were read—not of leaders, but of neighbors. People lost in hunger, in medical delays, in raids, in despair. Each name was followed by the toll of a bell, hand-forged from scrap metal, echoing across the square.

Tears streamed. But the silence did not feel like defeat. It felt like it was sharpening.

Grief had transformed into something heavier—resolve.

From Ashes to Resolve

One by one, voices rose—not from leaders, but from ordinary people.

- A farmer spoke of feeding his community despite raids.

- A nurse told of keeping patients alive when medicine was rationed.

- A mother described teaching her children barter and resilience instead of compliance.

Each story was a thread, weaving together into a tapestry of survival. From ashes, they declared, they would build—not under Boards, not under tyranny, but under their own resolve.

The vigil was not just remembrance. It was a blueprint.

The Firelight

As night deepened, torches were raised high. The square glowed as if aflame—not with destruction, but with determination.

Songs broke out, not written, but improvised, voices layering into rough, beautiful harmony. Children traced symbols in chalk at the edges of the square: circles for unity, broken chains for freedom, suns for new dawns.

The firelight reflected in eyes, not just of the defiant, but of the weary. Even those who had once complied stood with candles now. The breach had stripped away illusions. Only resolve remained.

The Presence of the Trustee

Though absent, perhaps imprisoned or vanished, the Trustee's presence was felt. Candles were clustered beneath murals painted of their likeness. Families whispered their words: *"Better removed for truth than honored for silence."*

Some swore they saw figures in the crowd—anonymous, cloaked—who may have been allies of the Trustee, spreading word of their survival. No one knew for sure. But the uncertainty only strengthened belief.

The Trustee had become more than a person. They were a symbol of resistance.

The Long Night

The vigil stretched deep into the night.

Food was shared. Blankets passed between strangers. Music lingered in the air, a rhythm of survival. Guards formed protective circles at the edge of the crowd, watching for patrols, but none came. Perhaps the Boards feared the people now. Perhaps they were too fractured to respond.

It was the first night in months where the people did not feel hunted. Instead, they felt present. Together. Unbroken.

The Dawn

As the first light crept over the horizon, candles guttered out. Torches dimmed. But no one left. They waited, faces turned east, watching the sky shift from black to gray to gold.

The sun rose not on the old empire, not on the Boards, not on the machine of control—but on something rawer, truer, unfinished.

The people stood weary, scarred, grieving. But they stood.

And in that standing was victory.

The Unanswered Questions

The vigil did not end with proclamations. It ended with silence. Everyone knew the questions still looming:

- Would the Boards strike back with force?

- Would new tyrants rise in the power vacuum?

- Would communities fracture again without a common enemy?

None of these questions were answered at dawn. But the people had resolved one thing: they would not return to chains.

The Vigil of Resolve was not the end of collapse. It was the beginning of what came next.

The Vigil of Resolve will be remembered not as the night the people won, but as the night they refused to lose. A night when grief hardened into defiance, when silence burned louder than slogans, when ashes became resolved—and when dawn revealed a world still broken, but no longer surrendered.

www.ingramcontent.com/pod-product-compliance
Lightning Source LLC
Chambersburg PA
CBHW021936190326
41519CB00009B/1037